Introduction to Application Security Vulnerability Information Management Strategy

Dr. Santanam Kasturi
Dr. John Pickard
Dr. Xiaolong Li
Dr. Peng Li

Title: **Introduction to Application Security Vulnerability Information Management Strategy**

ISBN: 979-8-89966-184-6

Author: Dr. Santanam Kasturi, Dr. John Pickard,Dr. Xiaolong Li, Dr. Peng Li

Cover image: https://pixabay.com/

Publisher: Generis Publishing
Online orders: www.generis-publishing.com
Contact email: info@generis-publishing.com

Generis
PUBLISHING

Introduction to Application Security Vulnerability Information Management Strategy

Santanam Kasturi[1], John Pickard[3] Xiaolong Li[2], Peng Li[3]

[1]Department of Technology Management, Indiana State University, Terre Haute, USA

[2]Department of Electronics and Computer Engineering, Indiana State University, Terre Haute, USA

[3]Department of Technology Systems, East Carolina University, Greenville, USA

CONTENTS

Preface

In an age where digital transformation shapes every aspect of organizational life, the imperative to safeguard information assets has never been more acute. The relentless march of technology brings with it not only innovation and opportunity but also an ever-expanding landscape of risk. Data breaches are no longer rare exceptions; they have become all too common, impacting businesses, governments, and individuals alike. These incidents exact a heavy toll, both in monetary terms and in the erosion of trust—a currency in today's interconnected world that is as valuable as any financial asset.

This book, Application Security Vulnerability Information Management Strategy, emerges from the pressing need to address the complexities inherent in managing the deluge of vulnerability data generated by modern software systems. As applications grow in scale, interconnectivity, and significance, the surface exposed to threat actors expands in parallel. Yet, it is not merely the existence of vulnerabilities that poses the greatest challenge, but the ability to detect, monitor, consolidate, and prioritize this information, transforming it from raw data into actionable intelligence that guides both defensive measures and strategic decisions.

Drawing upon decades of collective experience in cybersecurity, software engineering, and technology leadership, this text is designed as a comprehensive reference for practitioners, researchers, and decision-makers. Its purpose is twofold: first, to illuminate the state of the art in vulnerability information management—highlighting frameworks, technologies, and best practices; and second, to provide a pragmatic guide for organizations seeking to elevate their security posture in alignment with internationally recognized standards such as the NIST Cybersecurity Framework.

The content traverses the full lifecycle of application security vulnerability information, from discovery and consolidation to governance, metrics, correlation analysis, and beyond. Readers will encounter detailed discussions on emerging technologies, case studies, and the nuances of threat modeling, as well as actionable insights on incident response and business continuity. The intent is not merely to catalog technical solutions but to foster a security-minded culture that permeates every organizational layer, recognizing that technology, people, and processes are inseparable in the pursuit of resilience.

While the primary audience includes security architects, IT managers, cybersecurity analysts, and compliance professionals, this book also serves as a valuable resource for students and academics who aspire to understand the evolving dynamics of software security in practice.

It is my hope that the frameworks, methodologies, and lessons shared herein will inspire confidence, provoke thoughtful dialogue, and ultimately empower readers to meet the ever-shifting challenges of our digital era. In this landscape, vigilance must be constant, and knowledge—continually renewed—is our most potent defense.

Santanam Kasturi

Indiana State University, July 2025

Acknowledgements

This book would not have been possible without the help and support of my Co-authors, Dr. Xiaolong Li; Dr. John Pickard, and Dr. Peng Li. My sincerest gratitude and appreciation to you all.

This has been my dream, for a long time, to write a book and towards this effort I must recall the patience and personal sacrifices of my family members. Being my first book, I want to say this to my wife Sudha, my daughter Hamsika, and my son Ram that without your support, and understanding of how important this was for me, this effort would not have been possible. I am forever indebted to them, and the countless hours of my time spent on this work meant that I missed every minute of precious time I could not spend with you. For that I can only say, I owe you everything in my life. To my beloved parents, both of whom have not lived to see this moment, to see my first book, I hope I have made them proud. The same goes without saying to my father-in-law and mother-in-law who always treated me as their own son.

Chapter 1

Introduction

Chapter 1 - Organization, Structure and Key Components

Introduction

- Overview of rising digital threats and expanding attack surfaces
- Importance of proactive vulnerability management in digital environments

Defense in Depth (DiD)

- Definition and rationale for multi-layered security
- Eight primary security layers:
- Physical Security
- Network Security
- Endpoint Security
- Application Security
- Data Security
- Identity and Access Management
- User Security
- Policy Frameworks
- Benefits and challenges of DiD

Focus of the Chapter

- Distinction between general security controls and application security vulnerability management
- Emphasis on processes for managing vulnerability information rather than exhaustive technical controls

Key Themes

A. *Application Security Detection, Monitoring, and Identification*

- Role of application security platforms and automation
- Consolidation and management of vulnerability data

B. Application Security Vulnerabilities as Information

- Separating vulnerability data from sensitive business/personal data
- Protection, reporting, and awareness strategies

C. Application Security Vulnerability Information Management (ASVIM) Strategy

- Introduction to ASVIM and its importance
- NIST-recommended ASVIM components:
- Identify information requiring protection
- Record vulnerabilities from tests and scans
- Governance controls (access, training, data security)
- Monitoring and detection technologies
- Maturity models and metrics programs
- Operational threat intelligence and incident response
- Business continuity and incident recovery planning
- Legal and financial impact awareness

Summary and Key Takeaways

- Challenges of unremediated vulnerabilities and risk management
- Continuous improvement and adaptation of security controls
- Emphasis on awareness, governance, and a holistic security posture

Comprehension and Discussion Questions

- Questions reinforcing understanding of core concepts
- Prompts for critical thinking about application vulnerability management and organizational security strategy

1. Introduction

In the modern digital landscape, data breaches have become alarmingly frequent and costly, with attacks like ransomware often going undetected for weeks. These incidents can stem from a range of sources, including nation-states, organized crime, hacktivists, and even insiders seeking to exploit valuable information or demand ransom. The dramatic increase in such breaches is largely driven by the expanding 'attack surface,' which refers to every possible point where a system could be vulnerable.

As organizations connect more systems and increase digital interactions, it's critical they identify vulnerabilities, implement robust safeguards, and prepare to detect and counter even unknown threats. Effective response and recovery strategies are vital to limiting damage, as emphasized by Geer & McClure (2016, pp. 8-17).

Traditional approaches—relying solely on perimeter defenses—are no longer sufficient to counter today's sophisticated cyber threats. Instead, a multi-layered strategy known as Defense in Depth (DiD) has emerged as the standard. DiD involves placing several security barriers at different levels, making it significantly harder for attackers to succeed.

In essence, Defense in Depth is about layering protective measures—physical, technical, and administrative—across every facet of an organization. This approach covers physical security, network and endpoint protections, application and data safeguards, identity management, user education, and clear policies (Coole, 2012). By overlapping these layers, organizations build robust defenses that are much more resilient to attack.

While the book acknowledges the importance of DiD and data protection technologies, its main focus is on application security vulnerabilities—specifically, how to detect, monitor, consolidate, and effectively manage information about these weaknesses. It explores strategies for business recovery and addresses legal and reputational risks linked to security breaches.

This book introduces two essential themes:

- Application Security Detection, Monitoring, and Identifying Vulnerabilities: This section highlights the value of an application security platform capable of neutralizing threats, filtering out false positives, simplifying management, and automating detection and monitoring tasks. Whether using one comprehensive solution or a suite of technologies, the main focus is on the processes and information related to application vulnerabilities.

- Application Security Vulnerabilities as Information: Here, the importance of distinguishing sensitive data—like Personally Identifiable Information (PII), Protected Health Information (PHI), financial, and business data—from vulnerability information is discussed. Protecting sensitive data involves more than encryption or backup: organizations must know where this data resides, who accesses it, and how to detect misuse. Awareness and training are critical, as every user plays a role in maintaining security. The book details how to manage, report, and consolidate application vulnerability data, monitor key metrics, and improve remediation efforts.

While vulnerabilities can exist in both hardware and software, this book specifically addresses software application vulnerabilities. The persistence of unpatched weaknesses and poor software design are key contributors to successful attacks (Ciampa, 2019, pp. 12-13). Recognizing that not all vulnerabilities can be eliminated, the challenge becomes managing the risks of those that remain.

An effective Application Security Vulnerability Information Management (ASVIM) strategy is essential. ASVIM encompasses the extraction, transformation, storage, encryption, and management of critical data about application security weaknesses. In alignment with the NIST framework, an ASVIM strategy should include:

- Identifying what information requires protection
- Discovering vulnerabilities through tests and scans
- Implementing governance programs and controls, such as access control, awareness training, and data security
- Choosing and deploying monitoring and detection technologies
- Developing maturity models
- Establishing monitoring, testing, and scanning capabilities
- Building metrics programs for analysis and action
- Setting up operational threat intelligence and incident response capabilities
- Responding to and recovering from incidents
- Quantifying breach costs and developing business continuity and disaster recovery plans

- Understanding the legal impacts of inadequate action

Data breaches occur frequently, can result in significant costs, and are often discovered several weeks after an incident, particularly in cases involving ransomware. These breaches may originate from various sources, including nation-states, organized crime, hacktivists, and insider threats, all of whom seek information or ransom. The increase in data breaches is linked to a growing 'attack surface', which includes all possible exposures of an information system. As digital connectivity expands, organizations must address vulnerabilities, establish protective measures, detect previously unknown threats, and respond to and recover from incidents by mitigating risks (Geer & McClure, 2016, pp. 8-17).

As cyber threats become more advanced, organizations require multi-layered security rather than relying solely on basic perimeter defenses. Defense in Depth (DiD) is a strategic approach that applies multiple protection layers across systems, making it more challenging for adversaries to gain access.

Defense in Depth (DiD) is a fundamental cybersecurity strategy that emphasizes the deployment of several security layers to counter sophisticated cyber threats. This approach involves implementing controls across physical security, network security, endpoint security, application security, data security, identity management, user security, and policy enforcement (Coole, 2012).

DiD utilizes layered security controls—a combination of physical, technical, and administrative safeguards—to create obstacles that help protect sensitive data. Modern threats often exploit weaknesses across an organization's security environment, making this strategy relevant. The approach comprises eight primary security layers: physical security, network security, endpoint security, application security, data security, identity and access management, user security, and policy frameworks. Each layer addresses distinct aspects of security and adds redundancy to overall defenses. Effective implementation of DiD requires conducting risk assessments, applying a multi-layered methodology, and continuously monitoring to adapt to evolving threats. Advanced technologies such as machine learning and behavioral analytics can support detection and response. While DiD provides comprehensive security and enhanced incident response, it also poses challenges related to complexity, financial cost, and the necessity for continuous updates.

The central purpose of this book is not to provide an exhaustive explanation of Defense-in-Depth (DiD) or how to implement it. Extensive literature already exists on these topics. Similarly, this book does not focus on specific data protection technologies. Instead, it concentrates on issues primarily associated with application security vulnerabilities, examining strategies for their identification, monitoring, consolidation, and management. The book also addresses organizational recovery and response, outlining legal considerations and potential costs such as business losses and impacts on brand reputation.

This book highlights two key areas:

- **Application Security Detection, Monitoring, and Identifying Vulnerabilities**

This section focuses on the need for an application security platform capable of neutralizing threats, filtering benign activities, simplifying management, and improving efficiency through automation within the context of monitoring and detecting business applications. The platform may consist of a single technology or a collection of tools designed to address various aspects of application security. The discussion explores current detection and monitoring methods, with references provided. The aggregation and analysis of vulnerability information forms the core of this examination.

- **Application Security Vulnerabilities as Information**

This portion discusses the importance of distinguishing between Personally Identifiable Information (PII), Protected Health Information (PHI), financial data, business information (collectively categorized as sensitive information), and application security vulnerability information. While data security literature is extensive, safeguarding sensitive business data involves steps beyond encryption and backups—such as identifying data locations, monitoring access, and promptly detecting and responding to misuse. Security teams should promote user awareness and responsibility at all levels. Though general data security remains relevant, this book narrows its scope to "application security vulnerability information". Protecting such information relies on similar practices and tools used for other types of data. Key areas include identification of security information, establishing sharing and reporting controls, raising awareness, consolidating data for metrics, evaluating Key Performance Indicators (KPIs), and addressing vulnerabilities.

While vulnerabilities may occur in hardware and software, this discussion focuses specifically on software application security vulnerability information.

Successful attacks can result from widespread application vulnerabilities and software design flaws (Ciampa, 2019, pp. 12-13). Not all vulnerabilities can be remediated; therefore, managing unresolved vulnerabilities effectively is essential.

A structured Application Security Vulnerability Information Management (ASVIM) Strategy is important for organizations. ASVIM encompasses extracting, transforming, loading, analyzing, encrypting, storing, provisioning, and managing critical application security data. Following the NIST framework, the components of an ASVIM strategy involve:

- Identifying information that must be protected to reduce the likelihood of a data breach.
  - Recording vulnerability information identified via testing and scanning.
- Establishing governance programs with controls for access management, awareness training, and data protection.
- Selecting appropriate technologies for vulnerability detection and monitoring.
- Developing maturity models.
- Implementing ongoing monitoring, testing, and scanning processes.
- Constructing effective metrics programs for analytical and corrective actions.
  - Applying metric layers as required.
- Maintaining operational threat intelligence and incident response capabilities.
- Executing response and recovery procedures.
  - Assessing the financial impact of data breaches.
- Creating robust business continuity and disaster recovery plans.
- Understanding the legal consequences of failing to take adequate protective measures.

Summary

Overview of Application Security Vulnerability Information Management

Chapter 1 underscores the growing importance of managing application security vulnerabilities in a world where data breaches have become frequent, costly, and often go undetected for long periods. The expansion of digital connectivity has broadened the attack surface for organizations, increasing the need for robust security strategies.

The chapter emphasizes that merely focusing on traditional security layers—like physical controls or network defenses—is no longer enough. Instead, it highlights the concept of Defense in Depth (DiD), which requires multiple overlapping protections across all aspects of an organization's environment, including applications, data, identity, and policy controls.

However, the main focus of the book is not on general security measures or in-depth data protection strategies, but specifically on how to manage and safeguard information about application security vulnerabilities. This includes processes for detecting, monitoring, consolidating, and securely handling vulnerability data from tests and scans, while also protecting sensitive business and personal information.

Key components of an effective Application Security Vulnerability Information Management (ASVIM) strategy are outlined, including:

- Identifying which information must be protected to prevent breaches
- Governance programs that establish access controls, awareness training, and data security measures
- Implementing technologies for monitoring and detecting vulnerabilities
- Developing maturity models, metrics, and KPIs for continuous evaluation
- Setting up operational threat intelligence, incident response, and recovery plans
- Understanding the legal and business ramifications associated with breaches and vulnerability exposure

The chapter also stresses the importance of continuous improvement, employee awareness, and adapting controls as cyber threats evolve. Overall, Chapter 1 serves as an introduction to the book's central theme: building a comprehensive, adaptive, and secure strategy for managing application security vulnerability information.

Key Takeaways Essential

Insights from the Introduction

Key Points

- Escalating Threats: Data breaches are increasingly frequent, costly, and often go undetected for extended periods, resulting in significant risks from a wide range of threat actors.
- Expanding Attack Surface: The rise in digital connectivity has broadened organizational vulnerabilities, making robust security strategies essential.
- Defense in Depth (DiD): Effective security requires multiple, layered protections—spanning physical, network, endpoint, application, data, identity, user, and policy controls—to deter advanced cyber threats.
- Focus of the Book: While much has been written about DiD and data protection, this book centers on strategies for managing application security vulnerability information, rather than on general security measures.
- Vulnerability Management Strategy: Managing application security vulnerability information involves detection, monitoring, consolidation, secure handling, and mitigation—while safeguarding sensitive data such as PII and business information.
- Operational and Legal Considerations: The book covers business recovery, incident response, continuity planning, and legal ramifications related to data breaches and vulnerability exposure.
- Continuous Improvement: Effective vulnerability management requires ongoing evaluation with metrics, employee awareness, operational threat intelligence, and a commitment to adapting security controls as threats evolve.

Comprehension and Discussion Questions

For Application Security Vulnerability Information Management (ASVIM) Strategy

Comprehension Questions

- What are some of the main causes and consequences of data breaches discussed in the text?
- How does the concept of 'attack surface' relate to the increased risk of cyber incidents in modern organizations?
- Explain the principle of Defense in Depth (DiD) and list the eight primary security layers it incorporates.
- Why is Defense in Depth considered more effective than relying on single-layer security solutions?
- What is the central purpose of the book, and how does it distinguish itself from general cybersecurity literature?
- In the context of this discussion, what is meant by "application security vulnerability information" and why is it important to protect it?
- Outline the two key areas of focus in application security addressed in the text.
- What are the NIST-recommended components of an Application Security Vulnerability Information Management (ASVIM) strategy?
- Why can't all vulnerabilities be remediated, and what does this imply for organizations?
- List at least five essential tasks involved in managing application security vulnerability information according to the ASVIM approach.

Discussion Questions

- Discuss how expanding digital connectivity influences both opportunities and threats for organizations.
- Do you agree that layered security is necessary in today's threat landscape, or can organizations still rely on perimeter defenses? Why or why not?
- How do you think automation and advanced analytics can improve the detection and management of application vulnerabilities?
- In your opinion, what is the biggest challenge in protecting application security vulnerability information, and how might it be addressed?

- Consider the role of awareness training and governance in an organization's security posture. Can technical controls alone suffice?
- How should organizations balance the need to share vulnerability information for remediation purposes with the necessity of protecting sensitive details from malicious actors?

Chapter 2

Identifying the information that should be protected to prevent a data breach

Chapter 2 – Organization

Structure for Effective Discussion on Vulnerability Information Management

Introduction

- Significance of data protection in the digital age
- Impact of frequent data breaches and ransomware incidents
- Implications of a constantly expanding digital attack surface
- Defense-in-Depth (DiD) as a foundational security framework

Defense-in-Depth: A Multi-Layered Security Strategy

- Defining DiD and its fundamental principles
- Overview of security control types: physical, network, application, operational
- Necessity of overlapping and complementary controls
- Challenges such as complexity, cost, and evolving threats
- Role of continuous monitoring and regular risk assessments

Scope and Focus of the Chapter

- Emphasis on application security vulnerability information
- Distinctions between vulnerability data and other sensitive data sets (e.g., PII, PHI)
- Overview of the ASVIM (Application Security Vulnerability Information Management) strategy

Identifying Sensitive Information

- Types of sensitive organizational data: personal, health, test, vulnerability data
- Common threat vectors and associated risks
- Importance of effective data management and protection

Vulnerability Information in Application Security

- Key entry points for vulnerabilities (UI/web, API, source code, components)
- Mapping the attack surface and understanding organizational risk
- Analysis of the prevalence and impact of application vs. network vulnerabilities
- Illustrative exploit scenarios: authorization and authentication weaknesses

Consolidation and Storage of Vulnerability Data

- Benefits of aggregating vulnerability data from diverse sources
- Overview of key security testing and monitoring tools (SAST, SCA, API Security, DAST, Pen Testing, WAF, Hybrid WAF, RASP, External Threat Hunting)
- Database and data warehousing strategies for effective storage
- Risks and advantages of centralized information management
- Use of BI analytics and visualization tools for actionable insights

Summary and Transition

- Recap of main points covered in the chapter
- Preview of upcoming discussions: ASVIM strategy, NIST framework, and advanced management techniques

Comprehension and Discussion Questions

- Review and reflection questions to deepen understanding
- Discussion prompts focusing on practical application, risk management, and strategy optimization

2.0 Introduction

In today's digital age, data breaches occur frequently, often with significant financial and reputational consequences for organizations. Ransomware attacks, in particular, can go undetected for weeks and may originate from a variety of sources, including nation-states, organized crime, hacktivists, and even insiders. The dramatic rise in these incidents is largely due to the growing 'attack surface'—the totality of all points where an information system is exposed to potential threats.

As organizations embrace greater digital connectivity, they must be proactive in identifying vulnerabilities, implementing safeguards, and preparing to detect unknown threats. Effective response and recovery plans are essential to mitigate risks, as highlighted by Geer & McClure (2016, pp. 8-17).

Traditional perimeter defenses are no longer sufficient against today's sophisticated cyber threats. Defense in Depth (DiD) has emerged as a strategic approach, layering multiple defenses across systems to make it more difficult for attackers to succeed.

At its core, Defense in Depth involves deploying a series of security measures—physical safeguards, network and endpoint protections, application and data security, identity management, user training, and robust policies (Coole, 2012). By overlapping these layers, organizations create multiple barriers that deter attacks and help protect sensitive information.

This layered approach isn't just about technology; it also requires regular risk assessments, continuous monitoring, and the adoption of advanced detection tools like machine learning and behavioral analytics. While DiD offers robust protection and faster incident response, it also introduces challenges, including increased complexity, higher costs, and the ongoing need to adapt to new threats.

Although this book references the importance of Defense in Depth and related data protection technologies, its primary aim is to explore strategies for managing application security vulnerabilities. The focus will be on methods for detecting, monitoring, consolidating, and reporting on application security weaknesses, along with guidance on business recovery, legal considerations, and mitigating damage from breaches.

Readers can expect an in-depth look at two key areas:

- Application Security Detection, Monitoring, and Identifying Vulnerabilities: The discussion centers on building or selecting an application security platform that removes benign events, streamlines security management, and leverages automation for efficiency. While not endorsing any particular technology, the book reviews current detection and monitoring tools and the critical vulnerability insights they provide.
- Application Security Vulnerabilities as Information: This section distinguishes application security vulnerability data from other sensitive business information like PII and PHI. Protecting such data requires not just encryption and backups, but also knowing where the data resides, who accesses it, and how it is used. The goal is to foster awareness, consolidate data for better metrics, evaluate key performance indicators, and remediate vulnerabilities.

While vulnerabilities can exist in both hardware and software, this book specifically addresses software application security weaknesses. Not all vulnerabilities can be fixed, but the question remains: how can organizations effectively manage and prioritize those that are discovered?

The answer lies in developing a strong Application Security Vulnerability Information Management (ASVIM) Strategy, which involves extracting, storing, analyzing, encrypting, and controlling access to this critical information. The ASVIM strategy, aligned with the NIST framework, emphasizes a multi-layered defense that covers:

- Identifying sensitive information to prevent data breaches
- Governing access and training staff
- Adopting technologies for vulnerability detection
- Developing maturity models and robust metrics
- Integrating threat intelligence and incident response
- Ensuring business continuity and understanding legal impacts

The successful implementation of DiD requires continuous monitoring and risk assessments. Advanced tools such as machine learning and behavioral analytics are recommended to enhance detection and response capabilities. However, while DiD offers comprehensive protection, it also presents challenges, including complexity and cost.

2.1 Identifying the information that should be protected to prevent a data breach

As expressed before, there are several components to the critical organizational data. These include among many, sensitive personal data (personnel and customer), health information, functional test data used in validation projects, and security vulnerability aspect that contains the weaknesses in the organization's customer-facing applications. Some common threat vectors that are associated with these data sets include:

- All these data types need to be managed to protect the organization's assets and therefore the customer information.
- All face the threat of an external attack and insider exposure.
- All can cause a data breach that can be very expensive and hit the brand name.

Before we get into the ASVIM strategy and the NIST framework, the functional test data part of the strategy has been extensively covered in (Kasturi, 2020). While the other types of data are all critical to an organizational security posture, the focus of this book is to cover application security vulnerability information management strategy. The relevance and protection for other types of sensitive organizational information is covered extensively in available literature not referenced here.

The word information in this book hereafter is tied to only one entity – application security vulnerability information. Managing that information to enhance and protect an organization's security is what will be covered. Managing emphasizes that the information is discovered, and its impact of exposure is analyzed and understood end-to-end from source to target, from detection to remediation, from monitoring transaction traffic to monitoring controls. Identifying vulnerabilities, reporting, remediating, ensuring appropriate business and technology controls are in place, examining processes, people, and technology forms the rest of the discussion.

2.2 Vulnerability Information Discovered through Tests and Scans

In application security, vulnerability entry points are many – at the UI / web layer (URL and web application headers), at the Application Programming

Interface (API) layer (application to API, API-API), in the source code, and at the component layer (web services, micro services, REST services). This forms the exposed attack surface of an application, and an aggregate of all such exposed applications will provide an overall attack surface of an organization from an application security perspective. Some challenges do exist in handling such a large volume of data. In addition, according to the analysis performed on all vulnerabilities, the rate of critical vulnerabilities in the web application layer is approximately four times that of the network layer (Edgescan, 2019). Yet, most literature today reports studies on network-based intrusion detection systems (NIDS) than studies on web-based attacks (Sevri, 2019). Let us discuss how the vulnerability information discovered, listed in Table 1, through tests and scans can be exploited in a typical web application as shown in Figure 1 as an attack tree. The application used in Figure 1 is a web based, customer-facing internet application that allows access to look at products offered, get an online quote, and make an online purchase. The application also allows the user to look at policy information and update billing information. The user logs into the application using a web browser session, is authenticated, and authored to access documents and payment accounts for his user profile.

Assume there was an authorization error, and the user can look at other customer information, and specifically payment information (the transactions are shown by numbers in Figure 1), then the user (an attacker) can easily obtain, through social engineering, by calling customer service and obtain credentials to log in. This way the attacker accesses the real user's account and steals credit card information, using policy information (red lines) the user knows. Broken authentication, AP 12, is a weakness in Application Programming Interface (API's) that permits weak passwords for a user, and this can be exploited by an attacker by using credential stuffing which is another weakness associated with broken authentication AP 12 of the top 10 OWASP exploitable vulnerability (OWASP-API, 2023). The attacker can then log in to their authorized account and add another customer's credit card on file to make their account payment.

Figure 1

Attack Tree

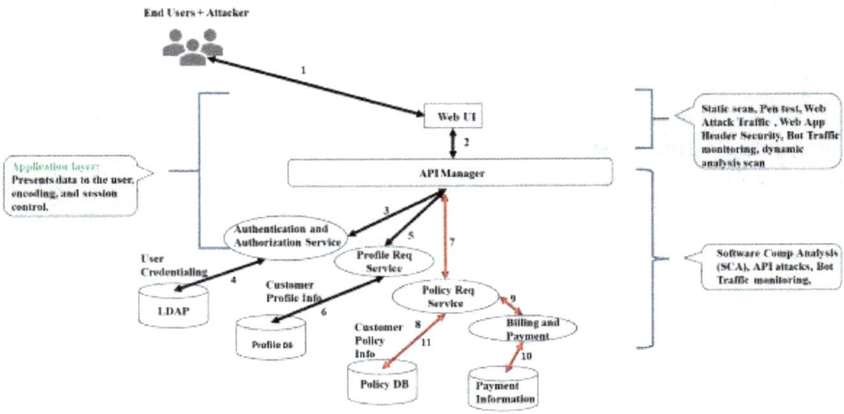

Fig. 1 Attack Tree

2.2.1 Vulnerability Information Consolidation in a database

Consolidating all application security vulnerability information from monitoring, detection, and discovery tools into a physical system allows for convergence of observation and response to an event that is a threat. Multiple application security testing and monitoring tools are deployed at different layers of an application architecture and capture activities that occur at that layer. Since web applications have become the primary targets of attackers with their widespread use nowadays, vulnerability data discovered through tests and scans must be treated as sensitive data that can provide an attacker with all information needed to cause data breach.

Table 1

Test / Scan Data

Capability	**Application Layer**	**Vulnerability Information**	**Alerts**
Static Analysis Security Testing (SAST)	Code	CWEs, Severity, Exploitability	Point in time scan reports
Software Composition Analysis (SCA)	Component	CVEs, Severity, Exploitability	Point in time scan reports
API Security	API	CVE's, CWE's, Severity, Exploitability	Point in time reports
Dynamic Analysis Security Testing (DAST)	URL/UI	CWEs, Severity, Exploitability	Point in time scan reports
Penetration Testing	URL/UI	CWEs, Severity, Exploitability	Point in time test reports
Web Application Firewall (WAF)	Deployed in front of the web app server	Blocked Attack Requests, Incoming threats	Continuous monitoring
Hybrid WAF	Deployed as an agent in the web app server	Blocked Attack requests, Incoming threats, target IP and host information	Continuous monitoring
Runtime Application Self Protection (RASP)	Deployed as an agent in the web app server	Blocked Attack requests, Incoming threats, target IP and host information	Continuous monitoring
External Threat Hunting	External Agency	Web header Issues, Ranking	Point in time reports

2.2.2 Data Storage

Data consolidation from multiple sources that reveal vulnerabilities at different layers of an application becomes a critical requirement to begin with. Without it, thinking about identifying an attack pattern, synthesizing an attack, or even predicting and preventing an attack will be fraught with risks of too many false positives.

Consolidating all types of vulnerability information in a single data warehouse and transforming the data into visualization models to be presented using a BI Analytics solution has specific advantages. The first advantage is the ability to correlate vulnerabilities discovered in multiple layers through multiple monitoring and detection capabilities. The second advantage is that one can make data-driven decisions quickly based on the highest risk score and prioritize the appropriate response. A conceptual data platform that gathers vulnerability from all the listed capabilities in Table 1 is shown in Figure 2. However, the downside is that storing all vulnerability information in one data store also raises the risk of attacks from external and internal threats and as a result the weakness in every application of the organization can fall into the wrong hands. All the test capabilities (Table 1) are used to test every weakness in this application. If the weaknesses that follow the red lines in Figure 2 are not remediated, and left exposed, an attacker can recon and exploit that very weakness and carry out the use case defined above. The point is this vulnerability information is stored in a database. The vulnerability information, if not managed well, is likely to be exploited!

Figure 2

Conceptual Vulnerability Information Platform

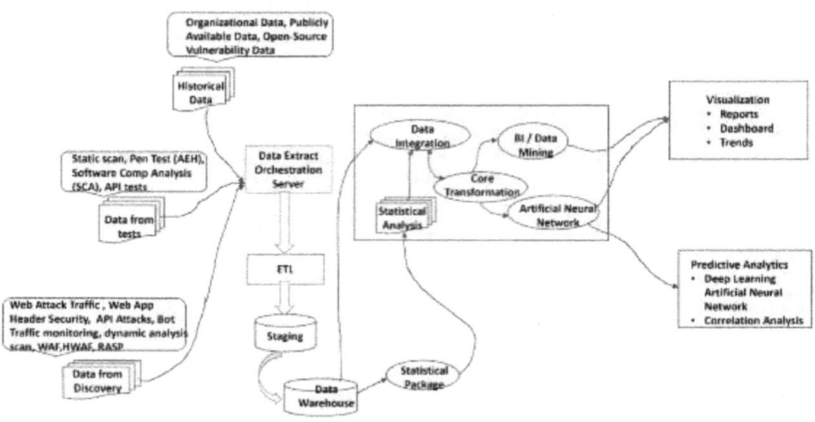

Summary

Consolidating and Securing Vulnerability Information

Chapter 2 explores the complex landscape of application security vulnerability information, focusing on the need for comprehensive consolidation and effective management. It begins by highlighting common exploit scenarios, particularly those involving authorization and authentication weaknesses, and underscores the importance of securing all types of sensitive data to prevent breaches.

The chapter outlines the diverse range of tools used to identify and monitor vulnerabilities, including SAST, SCA, API security solutions, DAST, penetration testing, WAF, Hybrid WAF, RASP, and external threat hunting. It emphasizes that vulnerabilities can be found at multiple application layers—from the UI and APIs to source code and components—each representing a potential entry point for attackers.

A central theme is the criticality of consolidating vulnerability data from these various sources into a unified database or data warehouse. Centralization enables organizations to efficiently correlate and analyze vulnerabilities, prioritize threats, and make informed, data-driven security decisions using robust BI analytics and visualization tools. However, the chapter also addresses the inherent risks of centralized storage, noting that a single repository can become a prime target for both external and insider threats.

Practical examples illustrate how attackers can exploit vulnerabilities if not properly managed, stressing the need for continuous monitoring, assessment, and timely remediation. The discussion sets the stage for the introduction of the ASVIM strategy and the NIST framework in subsequent chapters, with a strong focus on the effective management of application security vulnerability information as a cornerstone of organizational resilience.

Key Takeaways

- Defense-in-Depth (DiD) is essential: Implementing layered security controls—enhanced with continuous monitoring and analytics—offers robust protection against evolving threats but comes with complexity and cost considerations.
- Identify and prioritize sensitive data: Protecting critical organizational information such as personal, health, test, and especially application security vulnerability data is vital to avoid breaches and reputational damage.
- Application vulnerability entry points are numerous: Vulnerabilities span the UI/web, API, source code, and component layers, with the web application layer facing a disproportionately high rate of critical issues.
- Exploits often target authorization and authentication weaknesses: Attackers leverage errors and weak controls to gain unauthorized access, emphasizing the need for rigorous testing and timely remediation.
- Comprehensive testing and monitoring tools are required: A range of solutions—including SAST, SCA, API Security, DAST, Penetration Testing, WAF, Hybrid WAF, RASP, and external threat hunting—should be deployed to identify and manage vulnerabilities across all layers.
- Centralized vulnerability data management is powerful but risky: Consolidating all vulnerability information into a single database or data warehouse allows for advanced analytics and informed decision-making but creates a concentrated target for attackers.
- Effective management and remediation are critical: Vulnerability information must be continuously monitored, assessed, and remediated. Poor management may lead to data falling into the wrong hands and being exploited by attackers.

Comprehension and Discussion Questions

Understanding Consolidation and Security of Vulnerability Information

Comprehension Questions

- List three types of data that organizations must protect to prevent a data breach, as discussed in the text.
- According to the provided analysis, how does the rate of critical vulnerabilities in web application layers compare to those in the network layer?
- Describe the process by which an attacker could exploit an authorization error in a web application, based on the example given.
- What are the advantages of consolidating vulnerability information into a single data warehouse?
- What is one major disadvantage of storing all vulnerability information in a centralized database?
- Identify two types of reports or alerts generated by security testing tools listed in Table 1.
- What is the primary focus of the book as outlined in the transition to later chapters?

Discussion Questions

- Why is the consolidation of vulnerability information from multiple sources considered critical for organizational security?
- Discuss the potential risks involved in centralizing all vulnerability data in a single repository. How might organizations address these risks?
- How does the concept of Defense-in-Depth (DiD) enhance the security posture of an organization? What are the associated challenges?
- In what ways do different types of testing and monitoring tools (such as SAST, SCA, DAST, WAF, RASP) complement one another in vulnerability detection and management?
- What are some real-world scenarios where improper management of vulnerability data could lead to serious breaches?
- How does BI analytics and visualization improve the process of identifying and prioritizing vulnerabilities?

- What trade-offs should organizations consider when designing their vulnerability information management strategies?

Chapter 3

Establishing a governance program to implement controls

Chapter 3 - Organization

Governance and Controls in Application Security Vulnerability Information Management

Chapter Overview

- Introduction: Context for governance and control mechanisms in application security.
- Rationale for consolidating vulnerability data and adopting a governance program.

Centralizing Vulnerability Data

- Benefits of a centralized database
- Linking and analyzing vulnerabilities from multiple sources
- Enabling rapid, informed decision-making

Governance Program Fundamentals

- Defining the ASVIM Strategy
- Stages in planning, requesting, mining, masking/encrypting, and managing data
- Importance of stage-gating and oversight

Data Security Techniques

- Data masking: principles, advantages, and limitations
- Encryption: usage in production and non-production, risk mitigation, and impact on performance
- Maintaining referential integrity and validation
- Parallel testing and mutation analysis

Access Control

- Identity Management (IM), Authentication, and Authorization
- Active Control List (ACL) management and auditing
- Policy documentation for local and remote access
- Enforcing least privilege and separation of duties
- Protecting network integrity and implementing multi-factor authentication

Awareness Training and Insider Threats

- Role of education in reducing human error and insider threats
- Anonymous reporting channels and fostering a strong reporting culture
- Regular training and company-wide information campaigns

Physical and Administrative Data Security

- Physical protection of data centers
- Implementing cryptography, file screening, and WORM protocols
- Maintaining redundancy and strict authorization procedures
- Documentation of administrative procedures as SOPs

Best Practices and Framework Alignment

- Integration of NIST guidelines and industry standards
- Adapting controls to organizational needs and evolving threats
- Importance of audits and ongoing documentation

Comprehension and Discussion Questions

- Comprehension questions for review of key concepts
- Discussion prompts for application and critical thinking

3.0 Introduction

In today's digital era, where information flows freely and technology underpins nearly every business operation, the importance of robust governance and control mechanisms for application security vulnerability information cannot be overstated. As organizations collect, process, and store ever-increasing amounts of sensitive data, the risks associated with cyber threats and data breaches have escalated correspondingly. Effective management of vulnerability information—encompassing governance frameworks, centralized databases, secure data handling protocols, and rigorous access controls—forms the backbone of a resilient cybersecurity posture.

This chapter explores a comprehensive approach to application security vulnerability information management, grounded in the best practices established by the National Institute of Standards and Technology (NIST). It delves into the rationale and methodology for consolidating vulnerability data, the critical roles of governance programs, and the technical and administrative controls essential for safeguarding information assets. Through an examination of data security measures, authorization protocols, physical protections, and ongoing awareness training, we illuminate the multifaceted strategies organizations must adopt to protect their most valuable asset: information. By understanding and implementing these controls, enterprises can navigate the evolving threat landscape with confidence, ensuring both compliance and operational integrity.

Bringing application security vulnerability data together in a centralized database is essential for effective oversight. This approach allows organizations to link vulnerabilities found by different monitoring and testing tools, making it easier to analyze issues quickly and make well-informed decisions.

Establishing a strong governance program is fundamental for implementing necessary controls. A well-defined ASVIM Strategy guides the planning, requesting, mining, masking/encrypting, provisioning, and management of both test data and vulnerability information. Cloning production data is the most common method for preparing test datasets. Data masking and encryption are now vital for protecting customer privacy and sensitive information, and they stand as the most widely adopted techniques. Data masking, which is irreversible unless the process is both repeatable and consistent, can sometimes affect data validation—different outcomes may occur with each run. Even with consistent repeatability, referential integrity might be compromised, so care must be taken to maintain it. Masked data should always originate from production copies, and when refreshing, it's important to ensure that new production data meets the same validation rules as in testing. Parallel testing—using both unmasked production data and masked/encrypted data—can provide valuable evidence of data mutations caused by technical processes (Kasturi, 2020). This comparison also helps clarify the relationship between data mining, analytics, and data protection methods, ensuring reliability and integrity through repeatable tests.

Encryption is especially suited to protecting vulnerability data in production environments, while in non-production settings it acts as a risk mitigation tool. This is important when personnel have multiple roles (for example, a DBA who also tests), as unrestricted access could allow disruptions. However, encryption doesn't guard against insider threats or ransomware, and the choice of encryption technique can impact system performance—potentially causing delays or latency, particularly in testing situations (Kasturi, 2020).

A robust governance system should oversee all data requests, monitor their processing, and regularly review the status of both the requests and the provisioned data. Effective management requires people, processes, and technology at each stage, with clear checkpoints to detect and address any policy violations or security breaches. As outlined by the National Institute of Standards and Technology (NIST), best practices should be tailored to each organization's needs and operational context (Brumfield & Haugli, 2022, pp. 24–39). These practices include:

3.1 Access Control

Identity Management (IM), Authentication, and Access Control are all essential for restricting access to critical information so that only authenticated, authorized users can access what they're permitted to. According to the NIST framework, access to assets and facilities must be limited to authorized users, processes, or devices, and to approved activities and transactions (Brumfield & Haugli, 2022, pp. 24–39). Authentication verifies the true identity of a user, while authorization determines the specific resources and actions a user is permitted based on their role.

3.1.1 Key steps for access control include:

- Tracking who has system access, including when and from where—flagging cases such as employees accessing from abroad without approval, or ensuring that departing employees are deactivated from all systems by the end of their last day.
- Maintaining and auditing an Active Control List (ACL) that governs both physical and remote access, including for vendors and contractors, with legal safeguards to protect against liability.
- Documenting policies and controls for remote access, which carries additional risks. Remote users might misuse credentials or become victims to man-in-the-middle attacks on unsecured networks. Secure solutions like Virtual Private Networks (VPNs) and Software Defined Networks (SDNs) provide confidentiality and integrity, even over public networks (White & Donohue, 2014, pp. 188–189, 265–285; Kurose & Ross, 2017, pp. 408–416).
- Enforcing least-privilege access and separation of duties so that no single person has complete control over any function.
- Protecting network integrity through careful monitoring and controls for both internal and external communications. Network segregation is vital to prevent an attack from spreading between segments.
- Implementing multi-factor authentication so that breaching one layer of security won't automatically compromise the system.

3.2 Awareness Training

Insider threats, whether intentional or accidental, pose the greatest risk to organizations. Mistakes often result from a lack of awareness about cybercrimes, and even well-informed individuals may not always keep up with the latest threats. Sometimes, colleagues may notice red flags but say nothing for fear of retaliation. To address this, organizations can offer anonymous reporting channels, which have proven to encourage disclosures of suspicious or illegal behavior. Even if a report turns out to be a false positive, it's better to investigate, as organizations have dedicated resources to determine the truth.

External attackers also exploit insiders' lack of awareness or emotional vulnerabilities. Information awareness campaigns can help mitigate these risks. Essential actions include:

- Educating all employees about the potential impacts of cybersecurity incidents on business operations.
- Making cybersecurity a shared responsibility.
- Conducting regular training sessions.
- Providing clear guidelines for handling email, web browsing, social media, and mobile devices.
- Training employees to recognize and respond appropriately to potential cyberattacks.

The societal impact is also significant: for example, the 2013 attack on Target affected 110 million people, followed by similar breaches at Home Depot, Albertson's, Michaels, Neiman Marcus, P.F. Chang's, and Supervalu. As Hu (2014) noted, since cardholders are usually reimbursed for fraudulent charges, many people react to such news with indifference—but the underlying risks remain.

3.4 Data Security

Data is often the most valuable asset an organization owns and is therefore the prime target of malicious actors, especially databases full of critical business information. Following the NIST framework, organizations must consistently manage information to protect its confidentiality, integrity, and availability (Brumfield & Haugli, 2022).

3.4.1 Key steps for safeguarding data integrity include:

- Applying cryptography.
- Screening file-sharing activities.
- Implementing WORM (write-once, read-many) protocols to prevent unauthorized alterations or deletions.
- Maintaining both onsite and offsite redundancy for backup and recovery.

- Access should be strictly limited to authorized personnel for both usage and updates.

3.5 Authorization procedures must:

- Restrict administrative functions to selected individuals only.
- Document all user access levels to prevent policy violations.
- Ensure all administrative tasks and maintenance procedures are clearly documented as Standard Operating Procedures (SOPs).
- Finally, physical security is crucial. Data centers must be protected from unauthorized access at all times.

Summary

High-Level Recap of Key Aspects

This chapter emphasizes the importance of consolidating application security vulnerability data into a centralized database for streamlined management and analysis. It introduces the necessity of a structured governance program, detailing how to manage and protect sensitive data—particularly through data masking and encryption—to ensure privacy and security in both production and test environments.

The governance framework outlined covers:

- Access Control: Encompasses identity management, authentication, and authorization to guarantee that only approved individuals access critical systems, with policies for both local and remote access, least privilege principles, and network protections like segregation and multi-factor authentication.
- Awareness Training: Highlights the significance of ongoing security education to combat insider threats and human error, encouraging vigilance through regular campaigns, clear rules, and empowering employees to report suspicious activity safely.
- Data Security: Focuses on securing organizational data—especially vulnerability databases—by implementing cryptography, file screening,

write-once-read-many (WORM) protocols, redundancy, and stringent authorization and documentation procedures. Physical protection of data centers is also stressful.

Overall, the chapter presents best practices, aligned with guidelines from the National Institute of Standards and Technology (NIST), to ensure organizations establish robust controls, raise awareness, and safeguard their most valuable asset: data.

Key Takeaways

- Centralization of Data: Consolidating vulnerability information into a centralized database streamlines management, analysis, and rapid decision-making.
- Governance Program: A robust governance framework (ASVIM) is essential for planning, requesting, mining, masking/encrypting, provisioning, and managing vulnerability and test data. Stage-gating each process ensures effective rule enforcement and breach management.
- Data Masking and Encryption: These are key strategies for protecting sensitive information. Data masking is irreversible and must be consistent to preserve data integrity. Encryption is necessary in production and helps mitigate risk in non-production, though it cannot fully protect against insider or ransomware threats.
- Access Control: Identity Management, authentication, and least privilege access are critical. Access policies must cover both internal staff and external vendors, with controls for physical and remote access, and multi-factor authentication for enhanced security.
- Awareness Training: Regular training and awareness campaigns are necessary to combat insider threats and reduce the risk of human error. Encouraging anonymous reporting and fostering a culture of vigilance are vital.
- Data Security: Protecting the confidentiality, integrity, and availability of data—especially within databases—is paramount. Techniques include cryptography, file-sharing controls, redundancy, strict authorization, and physical protection of data centers.

Comprehension and Discussion

Questions For Deeper Understanding and Dialogue

Comprehension Questions

- What is the significance of consolidating application security vulnerability information into a centralized database?
- Describe the role of a governance program (ASVIM Strategy) in managing test data and vulnerability information.
- What are the main differences between data masking and data encryption, and what are their respective advantages and limitations?
- Why is stage-gating important in the process of managing data requests and provisioning?
- According to the NIST framework, what are the three main components required to restrict access to critical information?
- Explain the principles of identity management, authentication, and access control as outlined in the text.
- Why is it important to maintain and audit an Active Control List (ACL)?
- What risks are associated with remote access, and what technologies can help mitigate these risks?
- How does the principle of least privilege and separation of duty support better access control?
- What role does awareness training play in reducing insider threats and human error?
- List some examples of data security techniques mentioned in the text for protecting the integrity of databases.
- Why is physical protection of data centers emphasized as part of data security?

Discussion Questions

- Discuss how organizations can balance usability and security when implementing data masking and encryption for sensitive information.
- Reflect on a situation where insider threats could have been prevented by better awareness training or a stronger reporting culture. What steps could have made a difference?

- What challenges do organizations face when trying to enforce least privilege and strict access controls, especially with remote or third-party users?
- How can organizations ensure that their governance frameworks keep up with evolving security threats and technological advances?
- Consider the importance of regular audits and the documentation of administrative procedures. Why are these practices vital for maintaining data security?
- In your opinion, which component—technical solutions (like encryption), organizational processes (like governance and auditing), or human factors (like awareness training)—is most critical for robust application security, and why?

Chapter 4

Identify technology that should be implemented to monitor and detect Application Vulnerabilities

Chapter 4 - Organization

Structure and Flow of Key Concepts

Introduction

- Significance of application vulnerability monitoring and detection in modern IT environments
- Overview of essential strategies and technologies for organizations

Establishing a Metrics Program

- Importance of tracking vulnerabilities, closure rates, and security posture
- Role of metrics in prioritizing remediation and reducing risk

Developing a Maturity Model

- Introduction to BSIMM and SAMM frameworks
- Comparing internal and external assessments
- Table: Comparative Overview of BSIMM vs. SAMM

Monitoring, Testing, and Scanning Capabilities

- Layer-specific deployment of technologies (reference to visual figures)
- Overview of different testing and scanning types

A. Static Application Security Testing (SAST)

- Purpose and methodology
- Common vulnerabilities detected

B. *Software Composition Analysis (SCA)*

- Risks of open-source components
- Types of vulnerabilities uncovered

C. *Dynamic Application Security Testing (DAST)*

- Scanning operational applications
- Runtime vulnerabilities identified

D. *Application Ethical Hacking and Penetration Testing*

- Manual assessment beyond automated tools
- Types of weaknesses and system gaps revealed

E. *API Testing*

- Importance in distributed and modular systems
- Common API vulnerabilities and statistics

F. *Advanced Protective Technologies*

- Web Application Firewall (WAF): Function and use cases
- Hybrid WAFs and their evolution
- Runtime Application Self-Protection (RASP): Comparative strengths and real-time protection

G. *External Threat Hunting and Rating Agencies*

- Dynamic analysis by third-party services
- Impact of security ratings and public reporting

Summary

- Recap of essential strategies and technologies
- Emphasis on layered, metrics-driven, and maturity-focused approaches

Comprehensive and Discussion Questions

- Comprehensive review questions covering each section
- Discussion prompts reinforce understanding and application

4.0 Introduction

Safeguarding the Modern Application Landscape

In today's rapidly evolving digital ecosystem, applications have become both the cornerstone of organizational success and the focal point for sophisticated cyber threats. As businesses accelerate innovation and leverage complex software solutions, the challenge of safeguarding applications against a growing array of vulnerabilities intensifies.

This chapter delves into the essential strategies and technologies organizations must deploy to effectively monitor, detect, and mitigate application vulnerabilities. We explore why the establishment of a robust metrics program is foundational for informed decision-making and risk reduction and examine the critical role of layered security testing—from source code analysis to real-world penetration tests.

Readers will discover a comprehensive overview of static and dynamic testing methodologies, the importance of analyzing both proprietary and open-source software components, the unique challenges posed by APIs, and the transformative impact of advanced technologies such as Web Application Firewalls (WAF), Hybrid WAFs, and Runtime Application Self-Protection (RASP). Through this exploration, the chapter equips security professionals and technology leaders with the knowledge and tools necessary to build resilient, secure applications in an increasingly interconnected world.

Developing a robust metrics program is critical for effectively analyzing and responding to vulnerability information. This document highlights the necessity of tracking key indicators such as the number of vulnerabilities identified, closure rates, and the organization's overall security posture. A well-structured metrics program enables organizations to prioritize remediation efforts efficiently and minimize security debt. Despite comprehensive governance and controls, decision-making can remain disorganized without an effective approach to metrics.

4.1 Identifying Appropriate Technologies for Monitoring and Detecting Application Vulnerabilities

The testing and scanning capabilities outlined in Table 1, combined with ratings from external agencies and assessments at each application layer, ensure thorough coverage. Each capability should be deployed at specific layers of the application, as illustrated in Figure 1. Brief descriptions of these capabilities are provided below for reference.

4.2 Developing a Maturity Model

Begin with an evolving approach and, over time, incorporate industry best practices such as BSIMM or SAMM to achieve a self-regenerating model. Most organizations conduct ongoing internal assessments throughout the year; however, it is advisable to engage an external professional body with expertise across various industries. BSIMM serves as a descriptive measurement standard for software security, facilitating comparative analysis against industry peers. In contrast, SAMM offers a prescriptive framework with customizable practices suitable for organizations of varying sizes. While BSIMM is not a traditional maturity model, SAMM provides three defined levels and a clear starting point, as detailed in Table 2.

Table 2

Software Security Maturity Models

Comparing	BSIMM	SAMM
Primary categories	**Four high level domains** • Governance • Intelligence • SSDL Touchpoints • Deployment	**Five business functions** • Governance • Design • Implementation • Verification and Operations
Secondary categories	**Three practices per domain** • Governance • Strategy & Metrics • Compliance & Policy • Training **Intelligence** • Attack Models • Security Features & Design	**Three security practices per business function** • Governance • Strategy & Metrics • Policy & Compliance • Education & Guidance **Design** • Threat Assessment

Comparing	BSIMM	SAMM
	• Standards & Requirements **SSDL Touchpoints** • Architecture Analysis • Code Review • Security Testing **Deployment** • Penetration Testing • Software Environment • Config Mgmt. / Vuln Mgmt.	• Security Requirements • Secure Architecture **Implementation** • Secure Build • Secure Deployment • Defect Management **Verification** • Architecture Analysis • Requirements-driven Testing • Security Testing

4.3 Setting Up Monitoring, Test, and Scan Capabilities

Various types of scans are utilized by enterprises to protect their applications; these are briefly described below, with further detail available in referenced sources.

4.3.1 Static Analysis Security Testing (SAST)

Software development can introduce security risks. Prioritization of rapid development may result in overlooked security considerations, potentially leading to vulnerabilities. Research indicates that 83 percent of applications have at least one security flaw upon initial scan, and two out of three do not meet criteria based on the OWASP Top 10 and SANS 25. Additionally, over 74% of applications had at least one security flaw identified through a scan in the past year (Veracode, 2023). Among these, more than 69% contained at least one OWASP Top 10 flaw, and over 56% had at least one CWE Top 25 flaw (Checkmarx, 2022; Veracode, 2023; MITRE, 2022; OWASP, 2021; OWASP-API, 2023). SAST scans perform deep code analysis when the code is not running and before compilation, allowing identification of developer-introduced vulnerabilities. Common flaws detected via SAST include:

- Carriage Return Line Feeds (CRLF) Injection
- Cryptographic issues
- Information leakage

- Code quality concerns
- Credential management weaknesses
- Directory traversal
- Insufficient input validation
- Cross-site scripting (XSS)
- SQL injection (SQLI)

4.3.2 Software Composition Analysis (SCA)

Use of open-source components offers efficiencies but introduces certain risks. The share of open-source code in reviewed code bases increased from 36% in 2015 to 75% in 2020. Risks associated with known and unknown vulnerabilities, as well as compliance issues, may arise, such as zero-day vulnerabilities requiring rapid response. For instance, the SolarWinds breach highlighted the potential risks posed by malicious software libraries and the importance of governance (Carielli et al., 2021). SCA scans, often used alongside SAST, help identify additional vulnerabilities, including those reported in the NVD database and referenced by MITRE (2018). Frequently detected issues include:

- Information leakage
- Insufficient input validation
- Encapsulation issues
- Code injection
- Directory traversal
- Cryptographic weaknesses
- XSS
- SQLI

4.3.3 Dynamic Analysis Security Testing (DAST)

Unlike SAST, DAST scans analyze compiled code during runtime. They detect vulnerabilities present when the application is operational. Common issues found using DAST include:

- Server configuration problems
- Insecure dependencies
- Cryptographic issues
- Information leakage
- Encapsulation concerns
- Authentication issues
- Code quality deficiencies
- Credential management weaknesses
- Directory traversal
- XSS
- Code injection
- SQLI

4.3.4 Application Ethical Hack (AEH) / Penetration Test

An application ethical hack, or penetration test, involves authorized attempts to expose system vulnerabilities. These tests rely on the tester's expertise rather than automated tools and aim to identify areas where systems may be compromised. Typical testing activities include:

- Parameter manipulation and input validation assessment
- Attempting field manipulation and covert actions
- Testing for XSS, SQL injection, buffer overflows, and cookie weaknesses
- Identifying misconfigurations, patch management gaps, and other exploitable vulnerabilities
- Discovering information leaks due to inadequate storage or transit protections
- Assessing data center management practices and configuration processes
- Functionalities evaluated may include:
- Information protection
- Messaging
- Session token and timeout management
- Password management
- Backups
- Single sign-on mechanisms
- Integration with other systems and databases

- Additionally, such tests can reveal architectural shortcomings related to application design and coding practices.

4.3.5 API Testing

Application Programming Interfaces (APIs) are central to modern distributed software systems. As applications become more modular and reliant on APIs for communication, proper testing at this layer becomes essential. API security tests assess user access controls, encryption measures, and authentication mechanisms. The process simulates attack vectors to identify vulnerabilities and abnormal behaviors. According to surveys, 94% of respondents have experienced production API security issues, with top reported problems including vulnerabilities (41%), authentication issues (40%), and breaches (17%). Main vulnerabilities found through API testing include SQL and OS command injections, authorization/authentication bypasses, path traversal, and OWASP Top 10 API issues (OWASP-API, 2023; SALT, 2023).

4.3.6 Web Application Firewall (WAF) and Hybrid WAF

A web application firewall inspects HTTP traffic between a web application and the internet, filtering, blocking, or monitoring it as needed. Deployed at the network layer, WAF aims to protect against attacks such as SQL injection, XSS, and session hijacking. A WAF acts as a reverse proxy, filtering incoming requests according to defined rules. Its main advantages are its implementation speed and ability to update policies quickly (Akamai, 2023; Carielli et al., 2022).

Hybrid WAFs, discussed here in the context of external monitoring, expand on traditional WAFs by deploying within the web server and automating detection of a wider range of attacks. These may also operate as reverse proxies to protect legacy applications. Next-generation WAF solutions continue to evolve (Akamai, 2023; Signal Sciences, 2021; FASTLY, 2022). Run-Time Application Self Protection (RASP) extends these features by detecting application-level vulnerabilities during runtime (Na, 2021). While hybrid WAFs typically block transactions based on signatures, RASP tracks behavior to distinguish between normal and attack traffic (Signal Sciences, 2021; FASTLY, 2022).

4.3.7 Runtime Application Self-Protect (RASP)

RASP monitors applications in real time to identify code or configuration vulnerabilities during production, providing continuous monitoring and blocking of exploits. RASP expands upon hybrid WAF functionalities by analyzing transaction behaviors and distinguishing between normal operations and threats (FASTLY, 2022; Na, 2021).

4.3.8 External Threat Hunting Using Dynamic Analysis and Rating Agencies

Organizations may engage external services to monitor publicly accessible sites, identifying insecure headers or other issues. These assessments often result in scores or grades alerting organizations to vulnerabilities, which can affect reputation if made public (Shey, 2023; Morgan, 2021).

Summary

Key Strategies and Technologies

This chapter highlights the essential strategies and technologies organizations need to effectively monitor and detect application vulnerabilities. It emphasizes the importance of establishing a robust metrics program to track vulnerabilities, closure rates, and overall security posture, which guides prioritization and remediation efforts.

A maturity model, such as BSIMM or SAMM, helps organizations assess and improve their software security practices over time. The chapter outlines various testing approaches:

- Static Application Security Testing (SAST): Analyzes source code for flaws before compilation, identifying issues like input validation errors, cryptographic problems, and code quality weaknesses.
- Software Composition Analysis (SCA): Reviews open-source components for known vulnerabilities and compliance issues, highlighting risks from third-party and reused code.

- Dynamic Application Security Testing (DAST): Scans running applications to uncover runtime vulnerabilities in configuration, dependencies, and authentication mechanisms.
- Application Ethical Hacking (Penetration Testing): Simulates real-world attacks to expose exploitable weaknesses and architectural flaws, going beyond automated tools.
- API Testing: Focuses on the security of application programming interfaces, validating endpoints against vulnerabilities, authentication gaps, and data exposure risks.

Advanced protective technologies include Web Application Firewalls (WAF), Hybrid WAFs, and Runtime Application Self-Protection (RASP), each providing different layers of defense by monitoring, blocking, and reacting to threats at both the network and application levels.

Finally, external threat hunting—using dynamic analysis and security rating agencies—complements internal measures by identifying vulnerabilities in publicly accessible applications and providing benchmarks for improvement. These combined strategies enable organizations to build resilient, secure applications in an increasingly complex digital environment.

Key Takeaways

- Establishing a Metrics Program: Tracking vulnerabilities, closure rates, and security posture is essential for prioritizing remediation and improving decision-making.
- Adopt a Maturity Model: Frameworks like BSIMM and SAMM guide organizations to assess and enhance software security practices over time, tailored to their needs.
- Diverse Testing Strategies: Employ a combination of SAST, SCA, DAST, penetration testing, and API testing to detect vulnerabilities at different application layers and stages.
- Static Application Security Testing (SAST): Best suited for detecting developer-introduced flaws in source code before compilation.
- Software Composition Analysis (SCA): Identifies risks in open-source components, including known vulnerabilities and compliance issues.

- Dynamic Application Security Testing (DAST): Examines running applications to uncover runtime vulnerabilities in configurations, dependencies, and authentication.
- Penetration Testing: Simulates real-world attacks to find exploitable weaknesses beyond automated tools' reach.
- API Security Testing: Ensures application programming interfaces are secure from vulnerabilities, authentication issues, and data exposure risks.
- Use of Protective Technologies: Web Application Firewalls (WAF), Hybrid WAFs, and Runtime Application Self-Protection (RASP) provide layered defense by monitoring and blocking threats at network and application levels.
- External Threat Hunting: Engaging external agencies for dynamic analysis and scoring of internet-exposed assets helps organizations identify and address vulnerabilities before they impact reputation or operations.

Comprehensive and Discussion Questions

Comprehensive Questions

- What are the main goals of establishing a metrics program for application vulnerability monitoring? List the types of metrics organizations should track and explain their significance.
- Compare and contrast the BSIMM and SAMM software security maturity models. What are the key differences in their structure, approach, and applicability to organizations of varying sizes?
- Describe the primary function of Static Application Security Testing (SAST). What kinds of vulnerabilities does it detect, and at what stage of development is it used?
- Explain the purpose of Software Composition Analysis (SCA). Why has the use of open-source components increased risks, and what types of vulnerabilities can SCA identify?
- What distinguishes Dynamic Application Security Testing (DAST) from SAST? At which stage of application deployment is DAST most effective, and what are its strengths and limitations?
- Summarize the role of Application Ethical Hacking (AEH) or penetration testing. What unique insights can penetration testing provide that automated tools may miss?

- Why is API security testing increasingly important in modern application architecture? What unique vulnerabilities are associated with APIs?
- Discuss the differences between Web Application Firewalls (WAF), Hybrid WAFs, and Runtime Application Self-Protection (RASP). How does each technology contribute to application security?
- What are the benefits and limitations of engaging external threat hunting services for dynamic analysis and security rating of applications?

Discussion Questions

- How might an organization balance the need for rapid development and deployment with the necessity of robust security measures such as SAST, SCA, and DAST?
- As reliance on open-source components grows, what strategies should organizations adopt to ensure the integrity and security of their software supply chain?
- How do software security maturity models like BSIMM and SAMM help organizations move from basic to advanced security postures, and what challenges might they face in this process?
- In a multi-tiered, distributed application environment, how do API vulnerabilities differ from traditional application vulnerabilities, and what additional steps should be taken to secure APIs?
- Debate the potential advantages and disadvantages of using hybrid and next-generation WAFs versus traditional WAFs. In what scenarios might a RASP solution be preferable?
- With the evolving threat landscape, should organizations rely more heavily on automated tools or human-driven penetration testing for vulnerability detection? Justify your answer with examples.
- If an organization receives a poor security rating from an external agency,
- What steps should it take to address the findings and improve its public security posture?
- Reflect on a recent high-profile software security incident (such as SolarWinds). What lessons can be learned regarding vulnerability monitoring, detection, and the importance of layered security defenses?

Chapter 5

Setting up for Correlation Analysis

Chapter 5 - Organization

Structure for Correlation Analysis in Web Application Security

Introduction

- Overview of the importance of correlation analysis in web application security
- Objectives and scope of the chapter

Statistical Foundations and Tools

- Explanation of Pearson and Spearman correlation techniques
- Introduction to significance testing (two-tailed)
- Use of IBM SPSS for statistical analysis

Data Distribution and Preliminary Testing

- Discussion of the variability in valid attack requests across applications
- Description of the Independent Samples Kruskal-Wallis Test
- Application of the Kolmogorov–Smirnov Test for normality assessment

Classification and Data Preparation

- Traffic classification using Web Application Firewalls (WAFs)
- Collection and categorization of vulnerability data from various testing types (SAST, DAST, SCA, Penetration Testing)
- Data organization steps for subsequent analysis

Measurement Sequence and Analytical Process

- Identification of target applications and unremediated vulnerabilities
- Selection and classification of attack request types
- Mapping vulnerabilities to attack types
- Step-by-step application of correlation methods

Key Vulnerability Types

- Focus on Cross-Site Scripting (XSS), SQL Injection (SQLI), Path Traversal, Command Execution, and Backdoor vulnerabilities

Methodological Assumptions

- Explanation of variable selection and assumptions for correlation analysis
- Observation period and dataset parameters (e.g., 37 days, N=296)

Summary of Methodology

- Consolidation of the process for preparing and conducting the analysis
- Highlighting the multi-faceted testing approach and statistical rigor
- Emphasis on actionable insights and prioritization strategies

Comprehension and Discussion Questions

- Comprehension questions to reinforce understanding of methodology
- Discussion prompts to explore real-world implications and adaptations

5.0. Introduction

A Structured Approach to Statistical Evaluation of Web Application Security

In the multifaceted realm of web application security, understanding the intricate relationships between vulnerabilities and attack requests is essential for creating robust defenses. Correlation analysis stands as a powerful statistical tool, enabling researchers and practitioners to uncover hidden patterns, measure the strength of associations, and prioritize vulnerabilities that pose the greatest risk.

This chapter embarks on a structured journey through the methodologies and best practices of correlation analysis, focusing on the use of Pearson and Spearman techniques. Through careful selection of statistical measures, rigorous assumptions, and thoughtful data organization, we lay the groundwork for a comprehensive evaluation of security weaknesses. By leveraging advanced tools and analytical frameworks, such as IBM SPSS, we not only validate our findings but also illuminate pathways to more resilient application architectures.

As we proceed, each section will explore the nuances of measuring relationships within security data, the significance of data distribution, and the practical steps required to ensure reliable, actionable insights. The approaches detailed herein aim to empower both researchers and security practitioners to make informed, data-driven decisions in an ever-evolving threat landscape.

5.1 Preparing for Correlation Analysis: Statistical Approaches in Web Application Security

Chapter 5 focuses on the foundational steps for conducting correlation analysis within web application security. The primary statistical measures employed include the Pearson Correlation, Spearman Correlation (used as a non-parametric alternative when the dependent variable doesn't follow a normal distribution), and significance testing (two-tailed). These analyses are performed using IBM SPSS, which provides in-depth statistical insight (IBM, 2022; Warner, 2020).

It is important to recognize that the distribution of the dependent variable—valid attack requests—differs across all applications. This indicates that such requests are both random and specific, often targeted at particular applications. To evaluate this, an Independent Samples Kruskal-Wallis Test is conducted. This test helps determine whether the distribution of valid requests is indeed random and varies between the applications under study over the observation period.

Next, assessing if the dependent variable is normally distributed is accomplished via the one-sample Kolmogorov–Smirnov Test. If normality is confirmed, Pearson correlation is utilized. However, Spearman correlation is also applied in this research to reveal monotonic relationships between variables, even when normality is absent (Warner, 2020).

One of the advantages of correlation analysis is its capacity to reveal cross-correlations among vulnerabilities detected by various tests and scans. This is especially critical when managing many applications with hundreds or even thousands of flaws across an enterprise (Checkmarx, 2022). By identifying common vulnerabilities discovered by multiple testing methods, analysts can focus remediation efforts on unique vulnerabilities rather than redundant ones, thus highlighting the real targets for attackers.

The two core correlation focuses in this study are:

- Correlations among vulnerability types between different test methods.
- Correlations between valid attack requests and the associated vulnerabilities.

The first essential task is to classify web traffic as either known attack patterns or legitimate transactions. This is achieved today using Web Application Firewall (WAF) monitoring tools (Akamai, 2023; Carielli et al., 2022; FASTLY, 2022; Na, 2021; Signal Sciences, 2021). WAFs help detect anomalies in web requests, and application owners can fine-tune rules to optimize protection.

The second step involves collecting existing vulnerability data from point-in-time scans and tests of the same applications included in the study.

Both traffic classification and vulnerability discovery are detailed in Table 1, which outlines the capabilities for Static Application Security Testing (SAST), Dynamic Application Security Testing (DAST), Software Composition Analysis (SCA), Penetration Testing (also known as Application Ethical Hack testing, AEH), and Web Application Firewall (WAF). For more information, see

(Akamai, 2023; Carielli et al., 2021, 2022; MITRE, 2018, 2023a, 2023b; OWASP, 2021; Primeon, 2018; Veracode, 2023).

The third step is to organize the data for subsequent analysis. The fourth and final step is to apply either the Pearson or Spearman correlation technique (depending on data distribution), using IBM SPSS for comprehensive statistical analysis (IBM, 2022).

5.2 Measurement Sequence and Data Organization

The following four-step process should be followed:

- Identify the applications to be observed, preferably those that are internet-facing, have significant transaction volumes, and are critical to business operations.
- Identify all currently open vulnerabilities in these applications that have not yet been remediated, as determined by various types of internal testing (SAST, SCA, DAST, and Pen testing/AEH).
- Identify and select attack request types that show substantial transaction volumes—these can be monitored effectively by activating the WAF on the study applications.
- Identify vulnerabilities that correspond to these attack types, as described below, and focus observations on them.

5.2.1 Selection of Attack Request Types

Vulnerability information from the technologies listed in Table 1 informs this selection. However, for this study, each request and vulnerability category must be classified for inclusion in the observation and analysis. Based on surveys, the most prevalent application code vulnerabilities are selected (Kasturi et al., 2023; MITRE, 2018, 2023a, 2023b; OWASP, 2021; OWASP-API, 2023; Veracode, 2023):

- Cross-Site Scripting (XSS)
- Injection / SQL Injection (SQLI)
- Path Traversal (Directory Traversal)
- Command Execution

- Backdoor

5.2.2 Statistical Techniques, Assumptions, and Variables

This research utilizes both Pearson and Spearman correlation analyses. The underlying assumptions are:

- Dependent variables (attack requests) are continuous.
- Independent variables (vulnerabilities) are categorical.
- Observations are independent of one another.
- No significant outliers are present (Warner, 2020).

Observations for each variable were collected over a 37-day period (N=296). Kasturi et al. (2023) recommend extended observation periods and inclusion of multiple applications—potentially spanning different business lines and domains—to ensure consistency, reliability, and the ability to test for cross-domain effects and breaches of trust boundaries.

Pearson and Spearman analyses yield accurate results when dependent and independent variables are properly identified. Statistical measures applied include Pearson Correlation, Spearman Correlation (non-parametric for non-normal data), and significance (two-tailed) over large datasets (Warner, 2020).

Summary

Overview of Methodology and Steps

This section outlines the process for preparing and conducting correlation analysis on web application vulnerabilities and attack requests. The methodology involves:

- Assessing vulnerabilities across various testing types (SAST, DAST, SCA, Penetration Testing, and WAF monitoring).
- Classifying and gathering web traffic data to distinguish between attack and valid requests using tools like Web Application Firewalls.

- Organizing collected data for analysis, including identifying high-risk applications, recording open vulnerabilities, and mapping attack types to vulnerabilities.
- Applying statistical methods—Pearson and Spearman correlation—to measure relationships between valid request counts and identified vulnerabilities, as well as correlations between vulnerabilities detected by different test types.
- Employing statistical tests (such as Kruskal-Wallis and Kolmogorov–Smirnov) to ensure the suitability of data for correlation analysis.

The approach aims to identify significant patterns across applications, prioritize remediation efforts on unique vulnerabilities, and improve security by understanding how attack traffic correlates with existing weaknesses.

Key Takeaways

- Multi-Faceted Vulnerability Assessment: The methodology integrates various testing methods—SAST, DAST, SCA, Penetration Testing, and WAF monitoring—to thoroughly assess web application vulnerabilities.
- Web Traffic Classification: Web Application Firewall (WAF) tools are used to differentiate between attack and legitimate web requests, helping to identify anomalous activity.
- Comprehensive Data Organization: The process involves identifying critical applications, cataloging open vulnerabilities, mapping attack types to vulnerabilities, and focusing on high-risk instances.
- Statistical Rigor: Both Pearson and Spearman correlation analyses are employed, depending on data distribution, with supporting statistical tests like Kruskal-Wallis and Kolmogorov–Smirnov to validate assumptions.
- Insightful Correlations: The analysis explores relationships between the volume of valid requests and the presence of vulnerabilities, as well as correlations among vulnerabilities detected by different test types.
- Prioritization of Remediation: By identifying unique and high-impact vulnerabilities, resources can be focused on addressing the most significant threats instead of redundant or overlapping issues.
- Actionable Security Improvements: The approach enables organizations to better understand how attack traffic correlates with existing vulnerabilities,

ultimately guiding more effective security strategies and remediation efforts.

- Longitudinal Data Collection: Observations span a sufficient timeframe (e.g., 37 days, N=296) to ensure reliability and consistency in the patterns identified.
- Relevant Vulnerability Types: The analysis focuses on common and impactful vulnerabilities such as Cross-Site Scripting (XSS), SQL Injection, Path Traversal, Command Execution, and Backdoors.

Comprehension and Discussion Questions

Understanding the Methodology and Implications

Comprehension Questions

- What are the primary statistical methods used in the correlation analysis of web application vulnerabilities and attack requests?
- 2. Why are both Pearson and Spearman correlations employed in the methodology?
- 3. How is web traffic classified for the purposes of this analysis?
- 4. What role do Web Application Firewalls (WAF) play in the data collection process?
- 5. List at least three types of vulnerabilities that are a focus in this correlation analysis.
- 6. What are the four main steps outlined for preparing and conducting the correlation analysis?
- 7. How does the study determine whether to use Pearson or Spearman correlation for a given dataset?
- 8. Why is it important to organize the collected data before applying statistical methods?
- 9. What is the significance of conducting tests like Kruskal-Wallis and Kolmogorov–Smirnov in this research?
- 10. Over what period were the observations collected, and why is the length of this period important?

Discussion Questions

- How can understanding the correlation between attack requests and vulnerabilities help organizations prioritize security efforts?
- 2. Discuss the challenges and potential limitations of using correlation analysis in the context of web application security.
- 3. How might the findings of such a statistical analysis influence future security testing and remediation strategies?
- 4. In what ways could the methodology be adapted for different types of organizations or web applications?
- 5. Consider the implications of discovering that certain vulnerabilities are commonly detected by multiple testing methods. How should remediation strategies change in response?
- 6. What additional data or analytical techniques could enhance the accuracy and usefulness of correlation analysis in this field?

Chapter 6

Vulnerability Data from Vulnerability Chaining

Chapter 6 - Organization

Structuring Key Concepts, Processes, and Discussion for Effective Understanding

Introduction to Vulnerability Data and Threat Modeling

- Context of modern application security
- The significance of identifying and managing vulnerabilities
- Overview of attack trees and their role in security analysis

Constructing Attack Trees from Vulnerability Data

- Gathering vulnerability data (CWE, CVE, scans, WAF monitoring)
- Organizing and correlating weaknesses across applications
- Methods for building first-level and second-level attack trees
- Visualizing vulnerability linkages and exploitation paths

Metrics, Correlation Analysis, and Best Practices

- Comprehensive metrics and their value in vulnerability management
- Correlation analysis to reveal attack pathways
- Prioritizing remediation efforts and controlling security technical debt
- Fostering a security-minded organizational culture

Threat Modeling Methodologies

- Types of threat models: attacker-centric vs. software-centric
- Software-centric attack tree approach
- Step-by-step threat modeling process
- Mapping CWEs and CVEs to attack scenarios

Real-World Application: Data, Tables, and Attack Trees

- Tables mapping CWE and CVE relationships for various vulnerabilities (e.g., XSS, SQLI, CMDEXE, Path Traversal)
- First-level and second-level attack tree examples
- Overlaying real vulnerability data on threat models

Integrating Detection, Monitoring, and Response

- WAF and RASP integration for real-time detection
- Limitations and considerations in monitoring architectures
- Simulation exercises for risk assessment and resilience

Best Practices, Key Takeaways, and Cultural Transformation

- Effective governance and security-by-design approaches
- Proactive management of security technical debt
- Data-driven stakeholder engagement
- Resilience in complex, multi-application environments

Comprehension and Discussion Questions

- Questions to assess understanding of concepts and practice critical analysis
- Prompts for reflection on challenges, benefits, and continuous improvement in cybersecurity strategies

6.0 Introduction

In the rapidly evolving landscape of cybersecurity, the ability to identify, assess, and mitigate software vulnerabilities is more crucial than ever. Modern applications, interconnected through complex architectures and open-source components, are constantly exposed to a myriad of threats that exploit weaknesses both known and undiscovered. This document delves into the intricate process of managing vulnerability data, tracing the pathways that turn individual weaknesses into potential attack vectors, and constructing robust threat models to better understand and defend against these risks.

Central to our discussion is the concept of the attack tree—a visual and analytical tool that maps out how vulnerabilities interlink, revealing the multiple avenues an adversary might take to compromise an application. We explore the methodologies for developing and refining attack trees using real-world data, examining how unremedied flaws can propagate through systems and escalate security risks. By integrating insights from monitoring, detection, and correlation analysis, we demonstrate how organizations can not only visualize their current threat landscape but also prioritize remediation efforts and improve overall security posture.

Through a comprehensive review of vulnerability relationships, threat modeling processes, and practical frameworks for application security, this work aims to equip security professionals with actionable strategies to address security technical debt, foster a resilient security culture, and safeguard digital assets in an increasingly hostile environment.

6.1 Developing an Attack Tree from a Threat Model

An attack tree can be developed using the CWEs and the CVEs (from SCA) discovered through monitoring and detection methods through the parent-peer-child relationship of CWEs and CVEs that can identify a possible application-to-application spread of an attack. This can be further developed into a meaningful attack tree based on the application profile, equating to a threat model. The analysis from this research has shown how multi-application testing and monitoring can provide a view that vulnerabilities are not only correlated, but also linked (MITRE, 2018, 2023a, 2023b; OWASP, 2021). The included CWEs are from the latest 2021-2023 OWASP Top 10 and CWE Top 25 most dangerous software weaknesses lists in each case.

6.2 Insights from Metrics and Correlation Analysis

Data gathered from multiple detection and monitoring capabilities at different layers of an application using a time-series analysis will provide value and insights. Using the correlation analysis and the vulnerabilities identified as pathway to an attack, a vulnerability map-based attack tree can be developed using CWE and CVE information. This attack tree shows the linkages between vulnerabilities and a lineage pointing to how an attack could travel from the incoming WAF requests to deep down into the application code of exposed and existing, open vulnerabilities travelling laterally to create a more expanded attack. Some key insights that can be derived from metrics and how vulnerability data can be managed and organized is given below (Kasturi et al., 2024c):

- Development priorities and pressures lead to security debt piling.
- Vulnerabilities getting embedded in a spaghetti code.
- Linkages between vulnerabilities lead to an attack tree showing multiple pathways for an attacker.

Process improvements and evolving a maturity model solve the first two issues (Brumfield and Haugli, 2022; Geer and McClure, 2020; Glas, 2016). The following best practices are outlined in (Kasturi et al., 2024c).

- An effective security governance program ensures:
    - There are enough controls to protect all weaknesses.
    - There are monitoring and detection technologies to scan and report issues.
    - There exists full visibility of all existing issues and potential risks.
    - There exist effective remediation plans to plug gaps in controls.
- Security Technical Debt needs to be controlled.
    - A comprehensive metrics program will reveal a lot of unresolved vulnerabilities (Christopher, 2022). A security technical debt
- Security is a culture, a mindset!
    - For an effective remediation program, engagement with stakeholders must be a data driven conversation.

- The emphasis should be that security should be a mindset, an embedded feature in a development activity, not as an afterthought.
- Reactive chaotic fixes lead to the risk of a lost brand name or equity.

- An effective remediation program should demonstrate:
    - That application is reducing security debt.
    - An aggressive three-month closure rate is being pursued.
    - That 50% of flaws are closed in a quarter, rather than in two quarters, with all applications written in any language.

The third aspect requires data organization to develop an attack tree. Vulnerability data that is still unremedied is a dormant risk that can be exploited by insiders as well as outsider threat actors. As an outcome of this research, Kasturi et al. (2024c) propose the following sequence of tasks to organize data:

- Identify the applications that need to be under observation.
- Look at the vulnerabilities currently existing in these applications.
- Identify and pick the attack types in the form of requests.
- Identify the vulnerabilities that match with the attack types.
- Perform statistical and correlation analysis (Kasturi et al., 2023).
- Identify the CWEs and CVEs of all vulnerabilities of the applications included in the study.

6.3 Threat Modeling Process

Many organizations have started conducting simulation exercises that review the controls, gaps, and risk resiliency. The simulation and its effectiveness are continuously improving iterative study. The following needs to be in place before a simulation exercise can be performed (Hajrić et al, 2020).

- Identification of resources to be protected.
- Documenting the technical architecture
- Defining the security profile of the applications that details trust boundaries and data flow.
- Identifying the threats associated with architecture is a critical indicator (Xiong et al., 2022).
- Documenting the threats and their attributes

- Threat assessments, scoring the risk and impact, and cost of a breach.

Hajrić et al. (2020) propose two ways of applying a threat model.

- To design a system based on security architecture.
- To view all the pathways for attacks and assets being exposed.

Three types of threat models are in use in general:

- Attacker-centric method, which is focused on the attacker and the source of attack.
- Software-centric method, where focus is more on the data flow and the boundaries.

6.3.1 Software-centric Attack Tree method

The focus of the present research is application code. The software-centric method suggests looking at all vulnerabilities in the systems. A comprehensive threat model should look at infrastructure-based and application-based vulnerabilities. This is directly tied to the security debt. The next step in the process is to develop an attack tree to look at how vulnerabilities are spread across the enterprise. Figure 3 shows the threat model process and the attack tree.

6.3.2 Significance of the Attack Tree

Kasturi et al. (2024c) have proposed a method to develop an attack, from application vulnerability data discovered through tests and scans. Correlation analysis with incoming WAF requests needs to be analyzed to narrow down the focus to specific vulnerabilities and applications. The attack tree shows multiple pathways for an attack to evolve through vulnerability linkages. Relating to a parent, peer, or child CWE will provide more insight into the attack patterns. These patterns will reveal a multi-vulnerability, multi-application attack pattern which will be hard to visualize without data consolidation and correlation analysis.

Figure 3

Threat Model Process

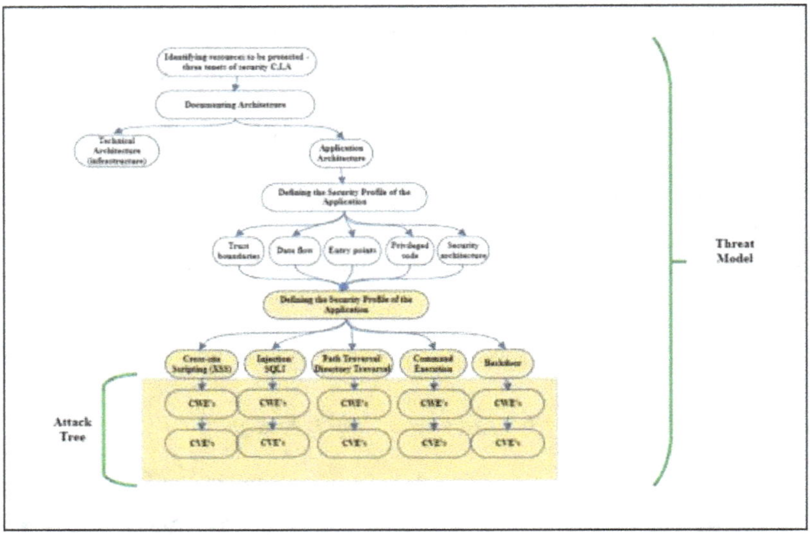

A traditional attack tree represents a set of assets that are in the path of a transaction visualized as a tree using a threat model (Lohmann et al., 2023; Saini et al., 2008). Threat modeling allows cybersecurity professionals to assess their security posture and evaluate potential risks to an organization's assets.

Use of a similar concept from known vulnerabilities and correlations established with incoming transaction requests monitored using a WAF is adopted in this research to develop an attack tree. Any transaction that passes through the tree will intersect with the vulnerabilities along that path and has the potential for an attacker to exploit those weaknesses in the application code. The concept proposed in this research is like the traditional attack tree that provides all the asset list (asset inventory) that forms an attack surface, and all the risks along the way for each asset with a known weakness.

Application topologies in an enterprise are distributed and connected with other applications, services, and databases within a business domain. Open-source components are shared among applications for ease of use and minimize development time. A globally accessible knowledge base of adversary tactics and techniques based on real-world observations is available. This knowledge can be used for developing threat models specific to each domain, depending on the asset topology and attack surface (Xiong et al., 2022). In its MITRE ATT&CK Enterprise Matrix, 266 techniques are listed as attack tactics, of which twelve are discussed in (Xiong et al., 2022) and listed below:

- Initial access
- Execution
- Persistence
- Privilege escalation
- Defence evasion
- Credential access
- Discovery
- Lateral movement
- Collection
- Command and control
- Exfiltration
- Impact

In a relatable sense to what has been proposed by Xiong et al. (2022), a conceptual model proposed in this research shows linkages between vulnerabilities in an application code and open-source component (Kasturi et al., 2024c). The attack tree presented in Figure 5 is based on observations in seven applications, five of which were only considered for a deeper analysis that had significant transaction requests seen by WAF tool (Kasturi et al., 2023).

6.4 First level Attack Tree

Inter-linking of unremedied vulnerabilities as a source-to-target vulnerability lineage, all linked through like a chain, shows multiple pathways for an attack. With hundreds of vulnerabilities, it is not easy to identify the specific threat patterns and pathways to a precise attack. Developing a vulnerability-based threat model and an attack tree resembling a vulnerability map is of value.

Table 3

CWE and CVE relationships for XSS vulnerabilities and request type

CWE	Parent of CWE	Child of CWE	Can precede a CWE	Can follow a CWE	Is a Member of CWE*	Is a peer of CWE / Can also be	CVE Mapping
79	80,81,83, 84,85,86, 87	74	494	113, 184	1337, 1347, 1387, 1425	352,494	CVE-2022-28599

Table 4

CWE and CVE relationships for SQLI vulnerabilities and request type

CWE	Parent of CWE	Child of CWE	Can precede a CWE	Can follow a CWE	Is a Member of CWE*	Is a peer of CWE / Can also be	CVE Mapping
89	564	943, 74		456	1337, 1347, 1387, 1425		CVE-2021-43408

Table 5

CWE and CVE relationships for CMDEXE vulnerabilities and request type

CWE	Parent of CWE	Child of CWE	Can precede a CWE	Can follow a CWE	Is a Member of CWE*	Is a peer of CWE / Can Also be	CVE Mapping
73	114	610, 642	22, 41, 59, 98, 434	399	1348, 1403 1337,		
77	78,88, 624, 917	74			1347, 1387, 1425		CVE-2022-26085
78		77		184	1337, 1347, 1387, 1425	88	CVE-2022-26085
79	80,81,83 ,84,85,8 6,87	74	494	113, 184	1337, 1347, 1387, 1425	352,494	CVE-2022-28599
89	564	943, 74		456	1337, 1347, 1387, 1425		CVE-2021-43408
94	95, 96, 1336	913, 74		98	1347, 1387, 1425		CVE-2023-22506

An attack tree from the vulnerability information is given below. The attack tree not only helps in focusing on the possible pathways to attack, but it also helps in creating simulation exercises along the same path as identified by an attack tree. The result of the simulation helps in prioritizing remediation efforts to eliminate the most vulnerable attack paths. The result of simulation also exposes inadequacies in coverage of monitoring and detection, gaps in controls, and a security technical debt that could be the root cause of much of the pain points. From Table 3, 4, and 5 a first level attack tree is developed, as shown in Figure 4. The attack tree is built from vulnerabilities listed in Table 3,4, and 5.

Figure 4

Attack Tree from CWE and CVE definition of XSS, SQLI, and CMDEXE

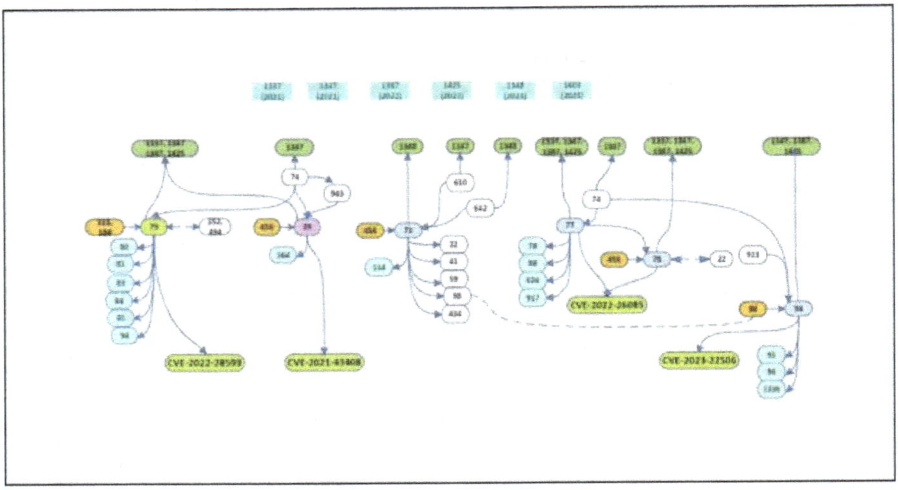

6.5 Second level Attack Tree

A second level tree as shown in Figure 5 can be developed by overlaying real vulnerability data from the applications into consideration. Figure 5 shows a real attack tree with existing open vulnerabilities shown in Table 6, 7, and 8.

Table 6

CWE and CVE relationships for existing open XSS vulnerabilities

CWE	Parent of CWE	Child of CWE	Can precede a CWE	Can follow a CWE	Is a Member of CWE*	Is a peer of CWE / Can also be	CVE Mapping
79	80		494		1337, 1347, 1387, 1409, 1425	352	CVE-2022-24891

Table 7

CWE and CVE relationships for existing open SQLI vulnerabilities

CWE	Parent of CWE	Child of CWE	Can precede a CWE	Can follow a CWE	Is a Member of CWE*	Is a peer of CWE / Can also be	CVE Mapping
22		20			1337, 1345, 1387, 1425		CVE-2022-38900, CVE-2022-23457, CVE-2021-37701, CVE-2021-37712

Table 8

CWE and CVE relationships for existing open CMDEXE vulnerabilities

CWE	Parent of CWE	Child of CWE	Can precede a CWE	Can follow a CWE	Is a Member of CWE*	Is a peer of CWE / Can also be	CVE Mapping
117					1337, 1347, 1387, 1425		CVE-2022-26085
611				184	1337, 1347, 1387, 1425		CVE-2022-40705, CVE-2021-33813
94					1347, 1387, 1425		CVE-2022-22965, CVE-2021-23337

A path traversal vulnerability CWE 22, child of CWE 20, with associated CVEs CVE-2022-23457, CVE-2021-37701, and CVE-2021-37712 is also included and shown in Table 9 and Figure 5. Although the authors (Kasturi et al., 2023) consider this as a weak correlation with incoming Traversal requests monitored by WAF, it is included as part of the existing vulnerability to build the attack tree.

Figure 5

Real Attack Tree developed from XSS, SQLI, and CMDEXE vulnerabilities found

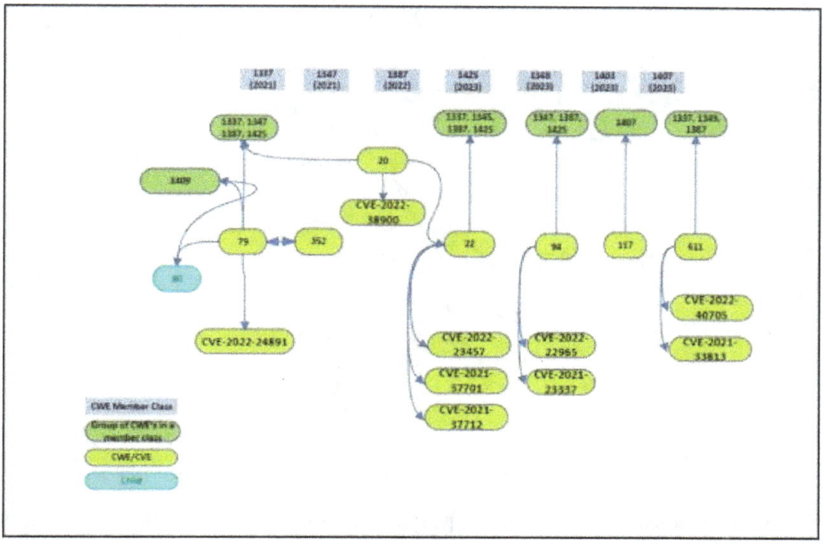

Table 9

CWE and CVE relationships for existing open Path Traversal vulnerabilities

CWE	Parent of CWE	Child of CWE	Can precede a CWE	Can follow a CWE	Is a Member of CWE*	Is a peer of CWE / Can also be	CVE Mapping
22		20			1337, 1345, 1387, 1425		CVE-2022-23457, CVE-2021-37701, CVE-2021-37712

Figure 6

Topology of an attack tree of a typical web application

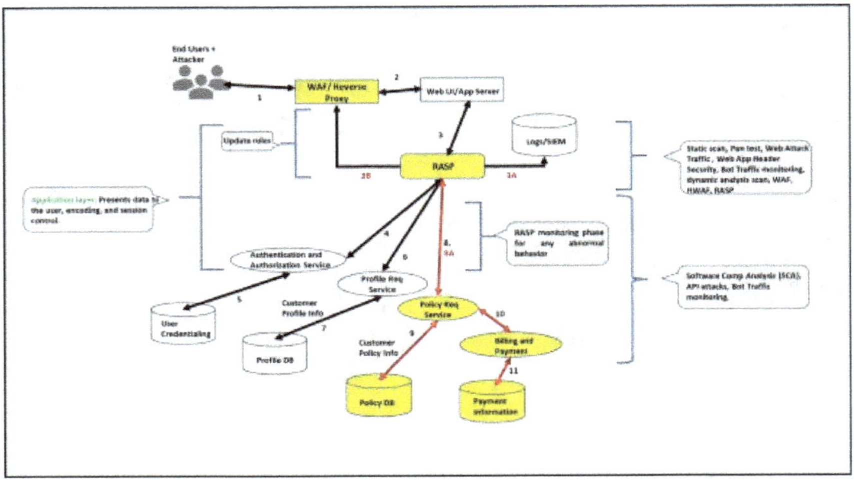

It is necessary how this all plays out together. The following sequence shows how this research was executed starting from monitoring and detection, based on the citations here (Kasturi et al., 2024a, 2024b, 2024c, 2024d):

- Monitor and detect vulnerabilities through tests, scans, and a WAF.
- Consolidate all the data into a single storage space for easy analysis.
- Apply correlation analysis for establishing a lineage between incoming requests and application code issues (vulnerabilities)
- Apply thread modelling methods to develop and attack tree.
- The attack tree is a representation of existing vulnerabilities leading to an attack path.
- Overlay the vulnerability map on a real threat model architecture.

An architecture for setting up a WAF-RASP threat intelligence system is proposed in (Salemi, 2020). The attack tree shown in Figure 1 is a template for a typical web application, a customer facing an internet application that allows access to look at products offered, get an online quote, and make an online purchase. Assume there was an authorization error that is detected by RASP as an abnormal behavior which allows the user to look at other customer's information, specifically payment information (the transactions are shown by numbers in Figure 6), then the user (an attacker) can, through social engineering, obtain credentials to log in. The modified attack tree (Figure 6) with the WAF and RASP combined in monitoring tracking a transaction departure from a normal behavior can trigger an alert. This can be ingested into an IR system for an appropriate response from the security operations team (Fastly, 2022; Na, 2021; Signal Science, 2021).

Summary

Key Concepts and Processes

This section explores how vulnerability data can be systematically managed and analyzed to strengthen application security. It introduces the construction of attack trees—visual models that map out how software vulnerabilities connect and can be exploited by attackers. Using standards like CWE (Common Weakness Enumeration) and CVE (Common Vulnerabilities and Exposures), these trees chart possible attack pathways across interconnected applications and components.

Key steps in the process include:

- Gathering vulnerability data through scans, monitoring tools, and WAFs (Web Application Firewalls).
- Organizing and correlating this data to reveal how unremedied flaws may link together, forming potential attack chains.
- Developing threat models and attack trees to visualize attack paths and prioritize remediation efforts.
- Overlaying real vulnerability data onto application architectures to produce practical, actionable attack trees.

The document also highlights best practices for reducing security technical debt, such as fostering a security-minded culture, emphasizing early remediation, and using comprehensive metrics programs to track and close vulnerabilities quickly. Real-world tables and examples demonstrate how mapping relationships among vulnerabilities assists in pinpointing and addressing the most critical security risks within complex software environments.

Key Takeaways

- Attack Trees Illuminate Vulnerability Chains: By systematically correlating vulnerabilities (using CWE and CVE standards), attack trees reveal how individual flaws can combine into exploitable attack pathways across multiple applications.
- Data-Driven Threat Modeling: Effective threat models overlay real vulnerability data onto application architectures, enabling organizations to visualize and prioritize the most critical risks for remediation.
- Security Technical Debt Requires Proactive Management: Development pressures often lead to unresolved vulnerabilities. Addressing security debt early and aggressively—such as closing 50% of flaws within a quarter—greatly reduces risk exposure.
- Comprehensive Metrics Are Essential: Collecting and analyzing vulnerability data across tools (scans, WAFs, monitoring) provides insights into trends, attack surface evolution, and the effectiveness of remediation efforts.
- Best Practices Drive Secure Culture: Establishing robust governance, adopting a security-by-design mindset, and engaging stakeholders in data-driven conversations cultivate a culture where security is embedded throughout the development lifecycle.
- Simulation Exercises Enhance Preparedness: Regularly simulating attack scenarios based on actual vulnerability data and attack trees helps identify gaps in controls and improve organizational resilience.
- Interconnected Application Risks: Attack trees and vulnerability mapping are particularly valuable in complex, multi-application environments, where open-source components and shared services can propagate risks laterally.

Comprehension and Discussion Questions

Assessing Understanding and Fostering Critical Analysis

Comprehension Questions

- What is an attack tree, and how does it help in understanding vulnerability chains within applications?
- How are CWEs and CVEs used to develop an attack tree according to the text?
- What role does correlation analysis play in mapping vulnerabilities to possible attack paths?
- Describe the process proposed by Kasturi et al. (2024c) for organizing vulnerability data to develop an attack tree.
- What are some of the best practices outlined for managing security technical debt?
- List the types of threat models mentioned and explain the primary focus of the software-centric method.
- Summarize the steps involved in executing a threat modeling process as described in the research.
- Using Tables 3, 4, and 5, what are examples of CWEs, and CVEs associated with XSS, SQLI, and CMDEXE vulnerabilities?
- How does overlaying real vulnerability data from applications enhance the development of a second-level attack tree?
- Explain how simulation exercises contribute to security posture and risk resilience.

Discussion Questions

- Why is it important to proactively manage security technical debt, and how might unresolved vulnerabilities impact an organization?
- In what ways can a culture of "security by design" improve remediation efforts and reduce risk exposure?
- Discuss the challenges and benefits of applying attack tree analysis in complex, multi-application environments with shared open-source components.
- How might comprehensive metrics and data-driven conversations with stakeholders transform organizational approaches to cybersecurity?

- Given the evolving nature of threats, how should organizations adapt their threat modeling and simulation strategies over time?
- What is the significance of mapping parent, peer, and child relationships among CWEs in anticipating attack pathways?
- Reflect on the value of integrating WAF and RASP into monitoring architectures for real-time detection and response. What potential limitations might exist?

Chapter 7

Building an effective metrics program for analysis and action

Chapter 7 - Organization

Structuring an Effective Software Security Metrics Program

This chapter is designed to guide the reader through the complexities of building, measuring, and maintaining a robust software security metrics program. To provide clarity and actionable insight, the chapter is organized as follows:

Introduction

An overview of the critical importance of application security, the evolving threat landscape, and the need for effective measurement programs to support resilience and strategic decision-making.

Establishing Metrics for Security Analysis

Discussion of the role that meaningful metrics play in identifying risks, managing vulnerabilities, and fostering a security-focused culture across the organization. The section opens with industry data, illustrates the impact of application complexity, and introduces foundational concepts such as security debt and the influence of programming languages.

Security Culture and Programmatic Foundations

Examination of the challenges of cultivating a security-oriented mindset and building processes that support proactive, organization-wide engagement in security initiatives. This section addresses common obstacles, including over-measurement, the balance between compliance and risk reduction, and the importance of actionable insights.

Measurement Myths and Practical Realities

A look at pervasive myths surrounding security metrics, with practical advice for overcoming barriers to effective measurement. The section includes a summary table comparing myth and reality, emphasizing scalability and continuous improvement.

Layered Metrics: Aligning with Organizational Roles

Breakdown of metrics by organizational level:

- Board-Level Metrics: Strategic, risk-focused measures and KPIs prioritized for leadership decision-making.
- Management Metrics: Operational performance, remediation rates, and security debt trends.
- Ground Truth Metrics: Technical and threat intelligence data for day-to-day operations and incident response.

Tables illustrate key questions, responses, and comments for each role.

Operationalizing Metrics and Tools

Survey of the technologies, processes, and frameworks that enable effective measurement, such as CI/CD integration, SIEM, SOAR, and threat intelligence platforms. This section also covers best practices for using standards like BSIMM and SAMM, with a focus on rapid detection, automated response, and the limits of technology alone.

Summary and Key Takeaways

A synthesis of the chapter's findings—emphasizing the importance of the SMART framework, continuous improvement, and the shared responsibility of security. A bulleted list of key lessons is provided for quick reference.

Comprehension and Discussion Questions

A section offering thought-provoking questions for review, reflection, and further group discussion, ensuring that readers can apply chapter insights to real-world scenarios.

This logical structure ensures that readers progress naturally from foundational principles through practical implementation, leaving them equipped to both understand and apply the tenets of a successful software security metrics program.

7.0 Introduction

In today's rapidly evolving digital landscape, the security of software applications has become a critical priority for organizations of all sizes. As technology advances and digital systems proliferate, so too do the risks associated with vulnerabilities, cyber threats, and data breaches. Effective security programs are no longer optional—they are fundamental to protecting sensitive information, maintaining customer trust, and ensuring business continuity.

This chapter explores the building blocks of an effective metrics program for analyzing and managing software security. Drawing on comprehensive industry data and best practices, it highlights the importance of cultivating a security-focused culture, outlines the challenges of measurement, and presents actionable strategies for organizations seeking to monitor and improve their application security posture. Through the thoughtful application of key metrics and continuous improvement, organizations can better anticipate threats, respond to incidents, and drive meaningful changes in their security operations.

7.1 Establishing an Effective Metrics Program for Analysis and Action

The State of Software Security (Veracode, 2023) report presents insights drawn from applications assessed through static analysis, dynamic analysis, software composition analysis, and manual penetration testing conducted on Veracode's cloud-based platform. The dataset, comprised of information provided by Veracode's clients, offers an in-depth perspective on trends and practices within application security from the viewpoint of code analysis.

7.1.1 Security as a Cultural Imperative

Over the past year, more than 74% of applications were found to possess at least one security flaw during their most recent scan. Specifically, 69% contained an OWASP Top 10 flaw, and over 56% had a CWE Top 25 issue. JavaScript applications exhibited fewer vulnerabilities—with just over half reporting flaws—while nearly 80% of Java and .NET applications contained defects. At initial scans, over 30% of applications showed vulnerabilities; this figure decreased to roughly 22% shortly after, before rising again to 30% over four years.

Applications older than four and a half years demonstrated an increase in new flaws, reaching approximately 35%. Application size also expands by about 40% annually, regardless of starting size. The choice of programming language greatly influences the prevalence and nature of vulnerabilities encountered, as well as the ecosystem of third-party libraries used. Java remains the predominant language analyzed by Veracode, constituting 44.2% of scans.

An effective remediation program includes:

- A focus on reducing accumulated security debt within the application.
- Implementation of an assertive three-month flaw closure rate.
- Achieving closure of 50% of identified flaws within one quarter across all languages, as opposed to extending remediation over two quarters.

Analysis of combined remediation and fix rates alongside the introduction of new vulnerabilities indicates a cumulative rise in application flaws over time. Some applications show no new vulnerabilities; however, this may result from infrequent scans or limited code changes necessitating rescans. Evaluating codebase size aids in identifying whether lack of detected flaws is due to stasis or genuine code quality improvements.

Integrating application scanning into CI/CD pipelines via API reduces the likelihood of vulnerability introduction by an average of 2%. Conversely, a 10% increase in application size correlates with a 0.6% increase in the probability of introducing additional flaws. Applications characterized by higher security debt—measured as one flaw per megabyte of code—are statistically more prone to future vulnerabilities. Increased scanning frequency is therefore critical to proactively identify and mitigate newly introduced vulnerabilities, thereby limiting the accumulation of security debt.

In conclusion, safeguarding against vulnerabilities requires not only technological solutions but also robust processes and active participation from personnel. With tools to assess application security exposures (see Table 1), pathways from weaknesses to exploitation (see Figure 1), and conceptualized data platforms (see Figure 2), it becomes essential to develop a comprehensive metrics program (Christopher, 2022).

7.1.2 Challenges in Measurement: Myths and Practical Approaches

Scalable application security programs, particularly for medium to large organizations, can be built upon fundamental principles. Assumptions should be continuously challenged through ongoing experimentation and iterative improvement. Regularly revisiting measurement controls ensures that metrics remain relevant and aligned with the organization's current security posture, as outlined in Table 10.

Table 10

Myths and Reality

Myth 1: Getting data is hard	Myth 2: Keeping data secure is harder, security is not for everyone	Myth 3: Takes too much time
Start with something, a minimal set of capabilities to detect and monitor, where you can get good data consistently and measure it.	Subjective measures based on expert opinion are bad. • Can you document something? • Can you count something? • Observe trends where you can. • Security is for everyone.	Optimize your constraints • Start with some team. • Do not boil the ocean. • Anything worth taking time and effort.

7.1.3 Cyber Security Responsibilities

It is important to determine whether someone is overseeing cyber security. Evaluation should focus on measuring security rather than solely compliance, as these areas may overlap but are not always aligned with the specific context.

Providing details suited to the situation is critical: for example, assessing not just the ability to run, but also the capacity to maintain a particular pace over time. The relevant question becomes, can the pace be sustained, such as maintaining 15 mph for 30 minutes?

- Metrics and Operations: Definition of Measure, Metrics, and Key Performance Indicator (KPI)
- Measure: Number of vulnerabilities

- Metrics: Find rate / Close rate – For example, how many vulnerabilities are identified during a scan in a given period, and how many are resolved?
- KPI: Closure to find rate – This refers to the ratio of fixed to found vulnerabilities during the same time frame.

7.1.4 Approaches to Measurement and Organizational Best Practices

Organizations are encouraged to foster a culture of measurement that supports informed decision-making by leadership. Before scaling efforts or assembling teams, it is advisable to confirm whether stakeholders require the metrics, even if they are presented as a checklist. There should be best practices ensuring that developing metrics is purposeful; each metric should have an associated cost and value. If not, organizations may need to revise their approach to metrics programs. One recommended method is to utilize the Specific, Measurable, Actionable, Relevant, Time-bound (SMART) framework along with supporting programmatic components, as referenced in Table 11.

Table 11

Meaningful measures

SMART	Programming Components
How many attacks do we see per day? – Specific	Monitor valid traffic.
How do we see those attacks, what tools, of what magnitude? – Measurable	Collect vulnerability data using tests and scans
What is the resolution course of action? – Actionable	Organize data, develop metrics, and KPIs for remediation of vulnerabilities.
Is it all garbage data, false positives? – Relevant	Analyze and compile data for usability.
What is the expected time of implementation, hours, days, weeks? - Time-bound	Report and consuming information – real time, near real time, or periodic as relevant.

7.2 Layers of Metrics as Applicable

Different levels within an organization require tailored information, and addressing these distinctions appropriately is crucial for securing organizational support. Metrics for the Board of Directors are typically developed by the Information Technology (IT) Leader, Chief Information Officer (CIO), and Chief Information Security Officer (CISO). At the management level, metrics are guided by the IT Manager, while operational metrics—ground truth data—are managed by IT Leads at the operational level. Each layer will be discussed briefly below and forms the foundation for constructing a maturity model aligned with industry's best practices. A comparison between two widely adopted Information Security models, the Building Security in Maturity Model (BSIMM) and the Software Assurance Maturity Model (SAMM), is provided by Glas (2020).

7.2.1 Board Metrics – Reporting to the Board of Directors

The Board evaluates organizational risk from multiple perspectives, considering both the implications of overcoming such risks and the impact on brand reputation and long-term business viability. By reviewing historical issues, strategies, and controls, the Board assesses their adequacy and identifies areas where new strategies may be necessary. They also examine the effectiveness of current measures, providing candid assessments of the organization's vulnerabilities. Governance practices within the security organization are often presented via dashboards, which may include external ratings, assessments, and benchmarking scores to facilitate peer comparison (Shey, 2023; Morgan, 2021). These tools enable the identification of pressing concerns requiring immediate action. Many organizations also conduct simulated threat exercises to evaluate their Business Continuity and Disaster Recovery responses (Barron, 2023; D'Hoinne et al., 2023). Consequently, the Board reviews specific metrics and Key Performance Indicators (KPIs) that reflect the organization's readiness and overall security posture, as outlined in Table 12.

Table 12

Board Metrics

Questions that an IT Security leader or CISO should be asking	Responses	Comments
Are priorities a factor in security debt?	Yes / No	If yes, does the security posture need reprioritization of program components to minimize security debt. If not, the causal factor for increasing security needs to be analyzed.
What is the security debt in terms of vulnerabilities discovered-to-remediation ratio?	• Global Annual - all applications • Global Monthly - all applications • Application Specific – annual and monthly	• Gives an annual KPI measured against an industry benchmark. • Gives a monthly KPI that shows a trend – are we getting better or not? • Gives how individual applications and the teams developing the code are doing. Provides a snapshot to leadership of poorly performing teams.
What is fix capacity?	Constant or variable	If a constant, clearly needs introspection. If no, then is there an improvement or is the security debt increasing?
Can we pry open security debt to get an insight?	Yes	Needs an application and team level analysis – does the team have experienced personnel, is the team following best practices, and if even security is a priority.
Does software security change by region?	Yes / No	Yes, if global rules are different from regional rules. There are different laws governing security for different countries. No, if there are certain business functions that require a common security module. The vulnerability and the exploitation factor are the same for every country.

7.2.2 Management Metrics – What do I tell the Chief Information Security Officer (CISO)?

A mature cybersecurity program must formally measure and report performance. As attack surfaces grow and digital technology expands, IT leaders—especially CISOs—face increasing pressure to show their impact beyond mitigating risk. They need to prove how security initiatives support organizational goals and identify which metrics best demonstrate this alignment (D'Hoinne et al, 2023; Lindstrom, 2022). Table 13 lists key metrics the CISO should know.

Table 13

Management Metrics

Questions that an Operational IT Manager should be asking	Responses	Comments
How prevalent are application flaws?	It depends on programming language and skills. A survey states 74% of applications have at least one security flaw found in the last scan over the last 12 months (Veracode, 2023)	Of the 74% more than 69% have at least one OWASP Top 10 flaw, and more than 56% have at least one CWE Top 25 flaw (OWASP, 2021; OWASP-API, 2023; MITRE, 2022)
What proportion of flaws are fixed?	Of the surveyed samples, 27% fixed more flaws than they discovered. About 49% found more flaws than they could fix (Veracode, 2019)	This excludes 24% who maintained a zero-balance for security debt.
How quickly are flaws fixed?	Survey points to 77% of flaws in third-party libraries (SCA flaws) remain open after the first three months, while only 57% of flaws found through dynamic analysis (DAST) remain open. The survey also reports 50% of flaws from static analysis (SAST) are closed within the first 290 days, while another 50% of the flaws from dynamic analyses	DAST flaws get remediated faster than SCA flaws, while the volume of flaws discovered through SAST are very huge and remain a daunting task to remediate all.

Questions that an Operational IT Manager should be asking	Responses	Comments
	(DAST) are closed in the first 143 days (Veracode, 2022)	
Does DevSecOps drive faster fixing?	DevSecOps does reduce typical fix timeframes by 72% and decreases overall security debt by five times (Veracode, 2019)	Adoption of DevSecOps still remains a challenge. The reason being technology integration and human resource challenges.
Is security debt rising or falling?	Security debt is aging and flaw accumulation over time, and about 50% of applications are adding debt over time, another 25% are driving it down, and another 25% maintaining a zero- balance.	Typically, teams fix new ones found and remediate the old ones as time permits. The old ones also get prioritized based on severity and likelihood of exploitation. This leaves many old flaws remaining open for many years,

7.2.3 Ground Truth "Metrics" – Operational Metrics

Threats vary in nature and do not all require identical responses. Analyzing the structure and origins of threats necessitates comprehensive monitoring, detection, and validation efforts. In recent years, certain threats such as malware, phishing, and credential abuse have consistently been among the most prevalent (D'Hoinne et al., 2023; Veracode, 2019; Veracode, 2022; Veracode, 2023). Allocating sufficient funding and resources to address these challenges is a significant consideration, as many breaches can be traced back to these types of threats. Determining appropriate levels of response and metrics for effective threat analysis remains a key issue. Table 14 provides a list of operational metrics that offer insights for identifying hidden threats. It should be noted that these are primarily application security vulnerability metrics. IT leaders, including CISOs, may consider:

- Evaluating the effectiveness of measures targeting top threats by monitoring deviations from established patterns to identify potential gaps in existing controls.

- Assessing the adequacy of the current security posture through ongoing monitoring and regular updates to policies, controls, standards, and strategies for future organizational security investments.
- Reviewing and prioritizing risks associated with emerging or uncertain threats, some of which may lack reliable data or result in false positives. Proper sorting based on relevance, urgency, attack feasibility, maturity, and the ability to measure remediation actions helps manage extensive vulnerability information and prevents misdirection.
- Considering non-technology threats, such as those originating from human behavior or insider activities that cannot be directly controlled through technical means. These situations often require process adjustments informed by qualitative metrics collected over time.

Table 14

Ground Truth Metrics

Questions that a Ground Truth data collection team should be asking	Responses	Comments
What is in scope, what is out of scope?	Only software applications, we do not include infrastructure application as part of the scope in this context.	Include internally accessible applications to take cognizance of insider threat.
What's external internet facing and what's internal facing?	Web applications that are externally and internally accessible.	All customer-facing applications are called external facing, and most applications catering to internal resources are called internal facing.
Where was this scanned or tested?	Testing can be of applications hosted on physical on-premises hosts and those hosted on a vendor cloud.	Some scan engines of application code exist in a vendor cloud (Veracode, 2023)
What are tools used?	SAST, DAST, SCA, Pen test, WAF, API tests, and External Rating Agencies	(Akamai, 2023; Carielli et al, 2022; Signal Sciences, 2021; FASTLY, 2022; Na, 2021; OWASP-API, 2023; SALT, 2023; Primeon, 2018; Carielli et al, 2021;

Questions that a Ground Truth data collection team should be asking	Responses	Comments
		Checkmarx, 2022; Veracode, 2023; MITRE, 2022; OWASP, 2021; OWASP-API, 2023, Shey, 2023; Morgan, 2021).
What are the applicable standards?	BSIMM and SAMM, (Glas, 2020), discussed in a later section.	One can engage consulting firms to do an evaluation of the current state and identify gaps to recommend improvements.
How many critical and high flaws did we find?	Measure of flaws by severity is an important metric to assess risk of exposure.	Discovered through all the tests and scans, this helps in reporting application weaknesses to the development teams
How many were carried over from last scan?	This gives us a measure of flaw aging, of how long these flaws have existed without remediation.	The ageing of flaws is a clear indication of time spent on remediation. Critical and high severity flaws remaining in the code need to be analyzed for dormancy, of whether they were found recently or were carried for a long time from previous code versions.
Overall, how many critical and high are pending resolutions?	Gives an indication of risk and impact	Set a threshold for risk acceptance and request a timeline or a compliance window for remediation beyond which these must be reported and escalated.
What is the remediation timeline?	Gives a timeline or a plan to remediate before the grace period for compliance expires.	If a remediation timeline is not given it means the flaws are not getting the right visibility and this needs to be reported.
Has something gone out of grace and out of compliance?	All out of grace period flaws become non-compliant with the accepted policy.	This needs to be managed as an issue for remediation.

Questions that a Ground Truth data collection team should be asking	Responses	Comments
Are there critical issues still unresolved?	Needs escalation for leadership visibility on the risks these issues pose.	No further deployment of the code can be allowed when the issue is past due to remediation.
What is the reporting format and frequency?	Electronic, dashboards, visualization, and analytics.	It can be daily, weekly, monthly, or even quarterly depending upon the value of information.
What are the data sources?	All the data that comes from each test, scan, monitoring, and rating tools	A composite data report needs to be presented for an overall assessment of the security posture.
Who is the responsible party to have found, and who is to remediate?	Everyone involved with the application.	Security is everyone's responsibility.

7.3 Setting up operational threat intelligence and incident response

Monitoring, detection, and protection measures cannot completely eliminate the risk of data breaches. No enterprise can fully guarantee a fail-proof security system. Therefore, incorporating threat intelligence and automated incident response is recommended for efficient response and recovery operations. Organizations maintain Business Continuity Plans (BCP) and Disaster Recovery Plans (DRP), which are initiated after an attack or breach occurs. The increasing volume of data and growing sophistication of cyberattacks underscore the importance of implementing automated threat intelligence feeds that aggregate information from multiple systems. Tools and processes such as Security Orchestration, Automation, and Response (SOAR), Cybersecurity Orchestration, Automation, and Response (XSOAR), Security Information and Event Management (SIEM), and Extended Detection and Response (XDR) offer automation, orchestration, and response capabilities to address security threats. Effective implementation and optimization of these technologies require an in-depth understanding of the solutions and the evolving market (Miller et al, 2016; Granadillo et al, 2016; Gibadullin & Nikonorov, 2021).

The data platform discussed in this paper for storing vulnerability information, when integrated with SIEM and SOAR/XSOAR, can provide—see Figure 7—with suitable customization and threat intelligence feeds such as Indicators of Compromise (IoC) (Reversing Labs, 2023).

Figure 7

Integrating Vulnerability Information, Threat Intelligence, SOAR/ XSOAR, SIEM, and EDR

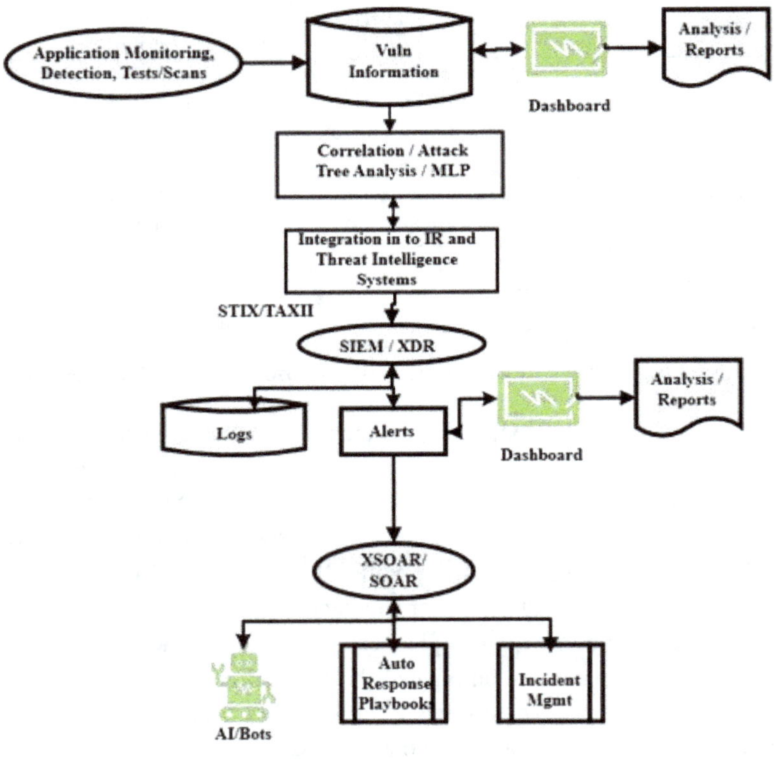

Summary

Key Insights and Practices

- This chapter discusses the critical importance of effective software security metrics programs in today's digital landscape. Using comprehensive industry data, it highlights the rising risks and vulnerabilities in software applications and the necessity of a security-focused culture. The text explains the challenges in measurement, dispels common myths, and stresses the value of starting with simple, actionable metrics.

- By adopting the SMART framework—Specific, Measurable, Actionable, Relevant, and Time-bound—organizations can develop meaningful measures to track security performance. The chapter breaks down metrics into three layers: Board-level (strategic risk and security debt), Management-level (prevalence and remediation of flaws), and Ground Truth (operational, technical metrics and threat intelligence). It emphasizes the importance of regular scanning, remediation, clear responsibility, and continuous improvement.
- Additionally, the use of modern tools like SIEM, SOAR, and threat intelligence platforms is recommended for rapid detection, response, and overall enhancement of security posture. Ultimately, the chapter advocates for a holistic approach that integrates people, processes, and technology to measure and strengthen application security effectively.

Key Takeaways

Essential Insights for Strengthening Application Security

- High Prevalence of Flaws: The majority of applications (over 74%) contain at least one security flaw, with significant numbers affected by critical vulnerabilities such as those listed in the OWASP Top 10 and CWE Top 25. Application size and language both influence vulnerability rates.
- Security Is a Culture: Building an effective security program requires fostering a security-focused mindset throughout the organization, involving people, processes, and technology.
- Importance of Measurement: Establishing meaningful metrics is essential. Use the SMART framework—Specific, Measurable, Actionable, Relevant, and Time-bound—to track and drive security improvements.
- Layered Metrics Approach: Different organizational levels require distinct metrics:
- Board-level: Focus on risk, security debt, and strategic KPIs.
- Management-level: Track flaw prevalence, remediation rates, and fix timelines.

- Operational level (Ground Truth): Monitor technical details, threat intelligence, and vulnerability trends.

Regular Scanning and Remediation: Frequent code scans, integrated into CI/CD pipelines, reduce new vulnerabilities. Prompt remediation and tracking of flaw aging are crucial for minimizing security debt.

Myth-Busting: Starting small, iterating, and optimizing measurement controls dispel common myths about the difficulty and inefficacy of tracking security data.

Advanced Tools and Automation: Leveraging solutions such as SIEM, SOAR, and threat intelligence platforms enables rapid detection, response, and improved incident management.

Continuous Improvement: Effective metrics programs are dynamic—revisited and refined over time to reflect the evolving threat landscape and organizational goals.

Shared Responsibility: Security is everyone's responsibility, with clear roles for detection, remediation, and reporting at all levels.

Holistic Security: The most effective programs integrate people, processes, and technology, aiming for continuous improvement and organizational resilience.

Comprehension and Discussion Questions

Comprehension Questions

- What are the main types of security flaws commonly found in applications, according to the Veracode report? How prevalent are these flaws across software?
- In what ways do application size and programming language affect the frequency and nature of vulnerabilities?
- What does the SMART framework stand for, and how can each component guide the creation of effective security metrics?
- Describe the three organizational layers of metrics (board-level, management-level, operational-level). What is the primary focus of each?

- How does integrating application code scanning into CI/CD pipelines improve the detection of vulnerabilities?
- What is "security debt," and how can organizations measure it?
- What kinds of questions should board-level leaders ask when reviewing software security metrics?
- Identify some common myths about measuring software security and explain the actual realities that counter these myths.
- How does DevSecOps contribute to minimizing security debt and reducing the time it takes to fix vulnerabilities?
- Which tools and standards are highlighted for collecting operational-level security metrics?

Discussion Questions

- How can organizations balance the need for comprehensive security metrics with the risk of over-measuring, which may divert resources from actionable improvements?
- Why is cultivating a "security culture" throughout an organization important, and what challenges might leaders face in achieving this goal?
- Should security measures focus more on meeting compliance requirements or on reducing actual risks and vulnerabilities? Why?
- In what ways does the growing size and complexity of applications make it harder for security teams to manage vulnerabilities?
- Evaluate the strengths and limitations of automated response systems like SOAR and SIEM. How should organizations supplement these tools?
- Given the persistent risk of insider threats, what combination of technology, processes, and organizational culture is most effective for identifying and managing such risks?
- How can organizations ensure that their security metrics remain relevant and actionable as technology, threats, and business needs evolve?
- What might happen if an organization fails to monitor and address security debt in the long term?
- How can security metrics and findings be clearly communicated to non-technical stakeholders, such as board members or executives?
- Reflecting on your own experience, what challenges do you anticipate when trying to build and maintain a sustainable software security metrics program?

Chapter 8

Response and Recovery

Chapter 8 - Organization

Safeguarding Organizations Amidst Cyber Threats

Introduction

An overview of the growing landscape of cyber threats and the importance of effective response and recovery strategies for organizations.

Understanding Cyber Threats

Describes the different avenues attackers can use, including data breaches, insider risks, and large-scale disasters, and highlights the importance of layered defenses.

Essential Security Practices

- Communicating business impact of cybersecurity incidents
- Making cybersecurity a shared responsibility
- Regular cybersecurity sessions and training
- Clear rules for digital conduct
- Training to identify and respond to attacks

Financial Impact of Data Breaches

Details on the costs of breaches, industry-specific impacts, and financial consequences of inadequate response.

- Rising average costs (with statistics from 2020–2023)
- Cost differences when involving law enforcement
- Sector-specific insights (e.g., healthcare industry)
- Mitigating factors and best practices (DevSecOps, employee training, incident response, threat intelligence)

Business Continuity and Disaster Recovery

Distinguishing between Business Continuity Plans and Disaster Recovery Plans, their processes, and their significance.

- Business Impact Assessment (BIA) and prioritization of services
- Components of DRP (evacuation, safety, backups, system shutdowns)
- Regular testing and plan updates
- Limitations of insurance coverage

Legal Ramifications of Data Breaches

Examine the consequences of breaches using case studies and legal updates.

- Case study: Equifax breach
- Common legal repercussions (lawsuits, penalties, business closure)
- Overview of evolving regulations, including notification laws and federal actions

Summary of Key Points

Highlights the holistic approach required, the importance of employee training, financial repercussions, and the necessity of proactive planning.

Comprehension and Discussion Questions

- Key concepts review on technical and non-technical measures
- Critical thinking prompts prioritizing response strategies
- Considerations for small organizations
- Debate current legal frameworks and organizational culture of awareness

8.0 Introduction

Safeguarding Organizations Amidst Cyber Threats

In an increasingly digital world, organizations face a growing spectrum of cyber threats ranging from data breaches and insider risks to large-scale disasters that can threaten business continuity. Chapter 8 delves into the essential strategies and practices necessary for responding to and recovering from such incidents. By examining modern security measures, the critical role of employee awareness, the financial and legal impacts of cyber incidents, and the importance of comprehensive planning, this chapter provides a roadmap for defending against attacks and ensuring swift restoration of operations when disruptions occur. Whether considering the staggering costs of breaches or the steps involved in business continuity and disaster recovery, this chapter equips readers with the knowledge to navigate the aftermath of cybersecurity incidents and to build resilience for the future.

8.1 Response and Recovery

There are multiple avenues through which attackers can access information. Addressing each type of attack with protective measures such as data masking and encryption is one approach. Additionally, protection through system upgrades and securing network perimeters using monitoring tools and services are important strategies. Insider threats and employee vulnerabilities constitute significant risk factors for organizations, which can be addressed through Information Awareness Campaigns. The following practices are considered essential:

- Communicating the potential impact of cybersecurity incidents on business operations
- Making cybersecurity a shared responsibility
- Conducting regular cybersecurity sessions
- Establishing clear rules for email, internet browsing, social networks, and mobile device use
- Training employees to identify and respond to cyber-attacks

8.2 Cost of Data Breach

In 2023, the average cost of a data breach reached USD 4.45 million (IBM, 2023), marking a 2.3% increase from 2022 (USD 4.35 million), and a 15.3% increase from 2020 (USD 3.86 million). Fifty-one percent of surveyed organizations indicated plans to increase security investments following a breach. One-third of organizations reported detecting breaches via their own tools and teams. Organizations not involving law enforcement incurred an additional USD 470,000 and experienced delays averaging 33 days longer. Healthcare data breaches in 2023 cost 53% more than those in 2020. Of the breaches, 82% targeted data stored in cloud environments. Adopting DevSecOps practices saved an average of USD 1.68 million; incident response planning and testing resulted in savings of USD 1.49 million (IBM, 2023; Donegan, 2022). Higher system complexity correlated with increased costs, with an added average of USD 1.44 million. Breaches lasting over 200 days resulted in higher expenses by USD 1.02 million compared to shorter breaches. Malicious attacks, particularly phishing and stolen credentials, accounted for 16% of initial attack vectors. Smaller organizations encountered proportionately greater financial impacts due to data breaches. Key mitigating factors among 27 studied include:

- DevSecOps
- Employee training
- Incident response planning and testing
- Incident response teams
- Encryption
- Security Information and Event Management (SIEM), Security Orchestration Automation and Response (SOAR), Extended Detection and Response (EDR)
- Proactive threat hunting
- Threat intelligence

8.3 Business Continuity and Disaster Recovery

Organizations facing potential financial losses from disasters implement business continuity plans (BCP) that inform disaster recovery plans (DRP). The primary distinction is that BCPs ensure ongoing business operations during a disaster, while DRPs outline recovery procedures to restore normalcy (Dobran,

2018). A business impact assessment (BIA) initiates the disaster recovery process, identifying priorities as follows:

- Critical: essential for organizational operation
- Necessary for normal operations: sustainable for up to 30 days before severe impact
- Optional: non-essential and restorable after 30 days
- Consider eliminating services identified as redundant over time

While BCP maintains business functionality at available capacity, DRP focuses on restoration and rebuilding and forms part of the BCP. Components of a DRP include evacuation plans, employee safety, backup protection, and systematic shutdowns to prevent further damage. Disasters may arise from various causes, including security incidents. Plans should specify steps to identify, isolate, protect, and recover systems, with regular testing to assure effectiveness (Conklin & White, 2010, pp. 505-506). Reliance on insurance in smaller organizations may reduce emphasis on BCP or DRP, though insurance may not cover all losses, such as:

- Financial losses (e.g., market share, fines, reduced profit)
- Reputational damage
- Legal challenges
- Contract breaches involving clients, vendors, or stakeholders (Kubasek, Brenna, & Browne, pp. 286, 2017)
- Delays in progress due to disaster impacts

8.4 Legal Ramifications

One example is the Equifax breach, where personal information of 143 million Americans was compromised during May–July 2017. The legal consequences included lawsuits, regulatory action, and increased oversight. Common legal repercussions for data breaches include (Data Privacy Group, 2019):

- Consumer lawsuits
- Criminal charges for regulatory violations
- Potential business closure

Regulatory requirements have become stricter, with updates to laws such as HIPAA and the introduction of new legislation like the Cybersecurity Information Sharing Act, Cybersecurity Enhancement Act, and Federal Exchange Data Breach Notification Act. These regulations aim to improve cybersecurity standards within organizations, ensure timely notification to consumers about breaches, and raise public awareness regarding cybersecurity risks (Alton, 2018; HIPAA, 2011). According to Smith, Gambrell, and Russell (2016), data breaches present both IT and legal challenges, requiring organizations to address:

- State notification requirements—All U.S. states, the District of Columbia, Guam, Puerto Rico, and the U.S. Virgin Islands have enacted data breach notification laws that require notifying affected individuals.
- Congressional actions, such as considering the Data Security and Breach Notification Act of 2015, which would mandate best practices for protecting personally identifiable information.
- Federal enforcement and litigation resulting from data breaches, which can significantly affect organizations

Summary

Key Points on Defending and Rebuilding After Cyber Incidents

Chapter 8 focuses on how organizations can effectively respond to and recover from cyber threats and incidents. Key strategies include not only technical defenses like encryption and system upgrades but also prioritizing employee awareness and regular training to address insider risks.

The financial impact of data breaches is significant, with average costs rising each year and the healthcare sector particularly affected. Effective measures—such as adopting DevSecOps, thorough incident response planning, and employee training—can significantly reduce breach costs. Organizations that do not involve law enforcement or lack coordinated response teams often pay higher costs and face longer recovery times.

Business Continuity Plans (BCP) and Disaster Recovery Plans (DRP) are critical for minimizing disruption and restoring operations. These plans begin with a business impact assessment to prioritize essential services and require regular testing to ensure readiness for both natural disasters and cyber incidents. Relying solely on insurance is risky, as it does not cover all losses, such as reputational damage and legal consequences.

The chapter also highlights major legal ramifications of data breaches, including lawsuits, regulatory penalties, and potential business shutdowns—using the Equifax breach as a notable example. Strengthened laws now require companies to notify affected parties and enforce stricter cybersecurity measures, making robust response and recovery planning more essential than ever.

Key Takeaways

- Holistic Cybersecurity Is Essential: Effective response and recovery after cyber incidents require a comprehensive approach that includes technical safeguards, system upgrades, and especially employee awareness to counter insider threats.
- Regular Training Reduces Risk: Ongoing cybersecurity education and clear policies for staff greatly mitigate risks and boost resilience against attacks.
- Financial Repercussions Are Significant: The average data breach cost reached $4.45 million in 2023, with costs rising annually and the healthcare sector being hit especially hard.
- Proactive Measures Save Money: Organizations that invest in DevSecOps, incident response plans, employee training, and robust technical tools can dramatically reduce the cost and impact of breaches.
- Delayed or Poor Response Increases Loss: Not involving law enforcement or lacking coordinated response teams leads to higher costs and longer recovery times after incidents.
- Business Continuity and Disaster Recovery Are Critical: Thorough BCP and DRP, starting with a business impact assessment and regular testing, are vital for minimizing disruptions and ensuring swift restoration of services.
- Insurance Alone is Insufficient: Relying only on insurance leaves organizations exposed to reputational, legal, and contractual risks that go beyond what insurance can cover.
- Legal Ramifications Are Severe: Data breaches can trigger lawsuits, regulatory penalties, and even business shutdowns, as exemplified by the Equifax incident. Laws now require prompt notification and stricter cybersecurity standards.

- Cybersecurity Is a Legal and Operational Issue: New regulations mandate both technical and procedural defenses, emphasizing that cybersecurity is not only an IT problem but a company-wide concern.

Comprehension and Discussion Questions

Exploring Key Concepts in Cybersecurity Response and Recovery

Comprehension Questions

- What are some of the key technical and non-technical measures involved in an effective cybersecurity response and recovery plan?
- Why is employee awareness considered critical in defending against cyber threats, especially insider threats?
- List three proactive actions organizations can take to reduce the cost and impact of cyber breaches.
- According to the data, what was the average cost of a data breach in 2023, and how has this amount changed since 2020?
- How do DevSecOps practices and incident response planning contribute to cybersecurity resilience?
- What are the differences between a Business Continuity Plan (BCP) and a Disaster Recovery Plan (DRP)?
- What is the role of a Business Impact Assessment (BIA) in disaster recovery planning?
- Why is relying solely on insurance not sufficient for organizations facing cybersecurity threats?
- Describe at least three potential consequences organizations might face following a major data breach.
- How have legal regulations surrounding cybersecurity evolved in response to incidents like the Equifax breach?

Discussion Questions

- In your opinion, which aspect of response and recovery—technical safeguards, system upgrades, or employee training—should be prioritized, and why?
- Discuss the challenges smaller organizations may face when implementing comprehensive cybersecurity policies and recovery plans.
- Do you think the legal obligations currently in place are sufficient to protect consumers and businesses from data breaches? Why or why not?
- How can organizations foster a culture of cybersecurity awareness across all levels of staff?
- Reflect on the statement: "Cybersecurity is not just an IT problem, but a company-wide concern." What does this mean in practice?
- What steps can businesses take to ensure their disaster recovery plans remain effective as technology and threats evolve?
- Consider a recent high-profile data breach (other than Equifax). What lessons can be learned from the organization's response and recovery process?

Chapter 9

CONCLUSION

Chapter 9 - Conclusion

Cyber-attacks continue at an alarming rate and far outpaced detection and resolution rates to overcome the impacts of such attacks. Advances in Machine Learning (ML) and neural network-based Deep Learning (DL) methods provide opportunities in application security to detect new variants of malware and zero-day attacks.

Data is the new oil and there is a tremendous marketplace for personal data and that has become the root cause of cybercriminals exploiting vulnerabilities. Historical data, a view of current trends, and future predictions give organizations and governments a view to focus on specific regions and threats targeting specific assets for attacks.

Sensitive data in a general sense is considered as customer or personnel information. This can be financial or health information. Data in the context of this book refers to application security vulnerability information found through security scans and tests of application code. Vulnerability information must be treated as any other critical organizational data. Consolidation of vulnerability data is necessary for rapid analysis and for performing correlation studies. It is recommended that data collection, data storage, and data analysis methods employ strict data security measures at rest and in transit as prescribed by NIST. Exploitation of vulnerabilities by a threat actor using weaknesses in application requires effort by the attacker. However, attacking the database that stores this information provides the attacker easy access to all vulnerability information in one data store. With little effort thereafter the attacker knows all the applications and their weaknesses to exploit in a more organized manner.

Vulnerabilities with higher severity and exploitability ratings are considered to pose higher risks. Application security data collection from tests and scans are always a point in time observations. However, vulnerabilities that are not remediated remain in the application for many weeks, and in some cases months, leading to exploitation. A remediation plan must be established to ensure high risk vulnerabilities are fixed as soon as possible. The challenge however is with open-source component vulnerabilities that have dependencies with all applications using the same component, so consuming a newer component with fewer vulnerabilities will impact dependent applications. This requires a strategy and governance to manage open-source components. In cases where remediation is difficult, or the development team feels it will take time, a mitigation strategy needs to be adopted.

CHAPTER 10

KEY TERMS AND DEFINITIONS

Chapter 10 - Key Terms And Definitions

Application Security Vulnerability Information Management Strategy (ASVIM): Is proposed as part of this work to securely store and protect the vulnerability information in the platform.

Attack Path: Is defined as the trail leading up to a weakness or vulnerability, linking other vulnerabilities creating a pathway for threat actor to exploit the application and the system.

Attack Tree: In the context of this research, it has been used to define multiple pathways for a threat actor to exploit weaknesses in multiple applications. In the traditional sense an attack tree is a collection of assets determined by a threat model as endpoints for an attack.

Attack Vector: Is the vulnerabilities and weakness in the application code that are seen as a threat potential for a threat actor to initiate an attack. These include commonly exploited vulnerabilities including, but not limited to, XSS, SQLI / Injection, Command or Code Injection, and Denial of Service (DoS).

Data Consolidation: Is defined in this research as monitoring, detection, and storage of vulnerability information in a secure platform for ease of use and reporting.

Data Security: Is a process to protect sensitive data, in the context of this research it means the vulnerability information discovered by the monitoring, testing, and scanning technologies.

Defense in Depth (DiD): Is a vital cybersecurity strategy that uses multiple security layers to combat advanced cyber threats. It ensures resilience through controls across physical, network, endpoint, application, data, identity, user security, and policies.

Detection: Is the method of identifying a weakness or vulnerability using a technology that will scan the code or test the application for exploiting vulnerabilities.

Monitoring: Is the technology that is stationed in the network or application layer to watch for incoming requests and identify their signature. A match with an established pattern or by behavior can reveal if it is a valid or malicious transaction.

Self-Regenerating: A system or process control that can pick up from where it broke to regain same state at which point it broke without losing any information, sequence, or corrections.

Severity: Is a rating and an associated score to emphasize the severity of an information security vulnerability. This helps in prioritizing remediation of vulnerabilities.

Threat Intelligence: Is an actionable process that through multiple technologies gathers attack patterns and threat alerts from multiple sources targeting multiple assets. This establishes a system that comprises issues being monitored, threat alerts from the issues, and alert feeds. These feeds are ingested into a threat response system. It is a combination of people, processes, and technology that intuitively responds to threats.

Threat Model: Is a structured representation of all critical assets requiring protection. The purpose is to identify absence of or inadequate controls and provide recommendations for testing the controls to assess risk and impact.

Weakness: Is a security flaw in an application code that can become an initial entry for a threat actor to probe but is not yet exposed. They are a potential risk.

Vulnerabilities: Are a collection of weaknesses that are exposed and can be exploited by a threat actor. They are a potential issue.

Vulnerability Map: Is a grouping of attack trees that have clusters of vulnerabilities chain linked with other vulnerabilities and applications crossing trust boundaries across domains.

AUTHORS

Dr. Santanam Kasturi

Santanam Kasturi has held distinguished positions in Science, Engineering and Information Technology as a Scientist, Visiting Professor of Physics, Release Manager, Test Architect, and presently as a Leader in the Information Security space. Santanam Kasturi obtained his Ph.D. from Indiana State University and has degrees in Master of Technology from National Institute of Technology, Karnataka, India, B.S in Engineering from Institution of Engineers, India, and a B.S in Physics, from University of Madras, India.

Dr. Xiaolong Li

Dr. Xiaolong Li is a professor in the Department of Electronics and Computer Engineering Technology at Indiana State University. He received his PhD in Computer Engineering from the University of Cincinnati in 2006. His primary areas of research include modeling and performance analysis of MAC protocol, Internet of Things, Wireless Ad Hoc networks, and sensor networks.

Dr. John Pickard

Dr. John Pickard is a professor of Information and Cybersecurity Technology at East Carolina University, North Carolina, USA. He received his PhD in Technology Management from Indiana State University in 2014. His main research areas are internet protocols, convergence of information and operations technologies, and Internet of Things applications.

Dr. Peng Li

Dr. Peng Li received his Ph.D. in Electrical Engineering from the University of Connecticut. His professional certifications include CISSP, RHCE and VCP. Dr. Li is currently an Associate Professor at East Carolina University. He teaches undergraduate and graduate courses in programming, computer networks, information security, web services and virtualization technologies. His research interests include virtualization, cloud computing, cybersecurity, and integration of information technology in education.

References

Akamai, (2023). Slipping Through the Security Gaps: The Rise of Application and API Attacks, *Akamai.*

Alton, L. (2018). 3 Repercussions of a Cyber Attack, Smart Data Collective, 2018.

Barron, K. (2023). 5 governance metrics boards should be watching ahead of proxy season, Diligent, *https://www.diligent.com/resources/blog/governance-metrics-boards-should-watch*

Brumfield, C., & Haugli, B. (2022). Cybersecurity Risk Management: Mastering the Fundamentals Using the NIST Cybersecurity Framework, Wiley

Carielli, S., DeMartine, A., Provost, A.C., & Dostie, P. (2021). The Forrester Wave™: Software Composition Analysis, Q3 2021-The 10 Providers That Matter Most And How They Stack Up, *Forrester August 2021.*

Carielli, S., DeMartine, A., Provost, A.C., & Dostie, P. (2022). The Forrester Wave™: Web Application Firewalls, Q3 2022, The 12 Providers That Matter Most And How They Stack Up, *Forrester, September 2022.*

Checkmarx, (2022). Correlation: The Application Security Testing Imperative in Modern Application Development, *Checkmarx*

Christopher, J. D. (2022). How to Mature ICS Security with Metrics, *Industrial Control Systems Security, 2022. https://www.sans.org/blog/mature-ics-security-with-metrics/*

Ciampa, M. (2019). Security+ Guide to Network Security Fundamentals, *6th Edition, Cengage*

Coole, Michael. (2012). Defense in depth, protection in depth and security in depth: A comparative analysis towards a common usage language, *December 2012, Conference: The Proceedings of the 5th Australian Security and Intelligence Conference, Perth, Western Australia*

Conklin, A. WM., & White, G. (2010). Principles of Computer Security, *McGraw Hill, pp.492-519.*

Data Privacy Group (2019). Data Breach: Legal Implications, *Data Privacy Group*

D'Hoinne, J., Watts, J., Furtado, P., Mirolyubov, E., Chugh, R., Khan, A., Zumerle, D., Thielemann, K., Voster, W., Walls, A., Gopal, D., Litan, A., Winckless, C., Hoover, J., Fazal, N., Allan, A., and Shoard, P. (2023). How to Respond to the 2023 Cyberthreat Landscape, *Gartner, ID G00786244, https://www.gartner.com/doc/reprints?id=12EGDN6DT&ct=230713&st=sb%20?utm_source=marketo&utm_medium=email&utm_campaign=Global-DA-EN2310097014u0000017jhoAAA-P3Unit42Unit422023gartner-cyberthreat-landscape-report*

Dobran, B. (2018). Business Continuity vs Disaster Recovery: What is the Key Difference? *IT Strategy, Data Protection, Disaster Recovery, Phoenix, NAP, 2018,* Available from: Business Continuity vs Disaster Recovery: What's The Difference? (phoenixnap.com)

Donegan, P. (2022). Preparing for New Incident Reporting Requirements, *HardenStance, Sponsored by Cyber Threat Alliance and Paolo Alto,*

EdgeScan, (2019). Vulnerability Statistics Report. *pp. 4-17, 2019. https://www.edgescan.com/wp-content/uploads/2019/02/edgescan-Vulnerability-Stats-Report-2019.pdf*

FASTLY, (2022).10 Key Capabilities of the Fastly Next-Gen WAF, *FASTLY, 2022*

Geer, D. E. Jr., & McClure, S. (2016). How to Measure Anything in Cybersecurity, *John Wiley & Sons, 2016*

Gibadullin, R.F., & Nikonorov, V.V. (2021). Development of the System for Automated Incident Management Based on Open-Source Software, *2021 International Russian Automation Conference (RusAutoCon)*

Glas, B. (2020). Comparing BSIMM & SAMM: Building Security In Maturity Model (BSIMM) compared to Software Assurance Maturity Model (SAMM)

https://owaspsamm.org/blog/2020/10/29/comparing-bsimm-and-samm/

Granadillo, G.G., El-Barbori, M., Debar, H. (2016). New types of Alert Correlation for Security Information and Event Management Systems. In Proceedings of the 8th International Conference on New Technologies, Mobility and Security, NTMS, Larnaca, Cyprus, 21–23 November 2016.

Hajrić, A., Smaka, T., Baraković, S., & Husić, J.B. (2020). Methods, Methodologies, and Tools for Threat Modeling with Case Study, *Telfor Journal. 12. 56-61. 10.5937/telfor2001056H*, Available from: Methods, Methodologies, and Tools for Threat Modeling with Case Study | Request PDF (researchgate.net)

HIPAA Research Guidelines and Information., (2011) *http://ora.research.ucla.edu/OHRPP/Pages/HIPAA.aspx*

Hu, E. (2014). I feel Nothing: The Home Depot Hack and Data Breach Fatigue

IBM. (2022). IBM SPSS Ver 29.0. *IBM Corporation North Castle Drive, MD-NC119 Armonk, NY 10504-1785 US,* Available from: SPSS Statistics 29.0.0 - IBM Documentation

IBM Security. (2023). Cost of a Data Breach, IBM Security. *Ponemon Institute and IBM Security*, Available from: Cost of a Data Breach Report 2023 (ibm.com)

IBM Security, (2023). Cost of Data Breach, *IBM Security, Study Conducted by Ponemon Institute, https://www.ibm.com/reports/databreach?utm_content=SRCWW&p1=Search&p4=43700077724064012&p5=e&gclid=Cj0KCQiAnrOtBhDIARIsAFsSe50xRrsxN_X0iygbYXBBRH4AahyBDU9tfFZPWxi9ZUk7Fb6GfaVeqtgaAkBGEALw_wcB&gclsrc=aw.ds*

Kasturi, S. (2020). Some Aspects of Test Data Management Strategy, *2020 IEEE International Conference on Computing, Power and Communication Technologies (GUCON), Galgotias University, Greater Noida, UP, India. Oct 2-4, 2020*

Kasturi, S., Li, X., Pickard, J., & Li, P. (2023). Understanding Statistical Correlation of Application Security Vulnerability Data from Detection and Monitoring Tools. In Proceedings of the *2023 33rd International*

Telecommunication Networks and Applications Conference, Melbourne, Australia, 2023, pp. 289-296, Available from: https://doi.org/10.1109/ITNAC59571.2023.10368476

Kasturi, S., Li, X., Li, P., & Pickard, J. (2024a). On the Benefits of Vulnerability Data Consolidation in Application Security. Vol. 19 No. 1 (2024): In Proceedings of the *19th International Conference on Cyber Warfare and Security, pp. 455-462*, Available from: https://doi.org/10.34190/iccws.19.1.2086

Kasturi, S., Li, X., Li, P., & Pickard, J. (2024b). A Proposed Approach to Integrate Application Security Vulnerability Data with Incidence Response Systems. In *American Journal of Networks and Communications, 13(1), 19-29*, Available from: https://doi.org/10.11648/j.ajnc.20241301.12

Kasturi, S., Li, X., Pickard, J., & Li, P. (2024c). Prioritization of Application Security Vulnerability Remediation Using Metrics, Correlation Analysis, and Threat Model. In *American Journal of Software Engineering and Applications, 12(1), 5-13,* Available from: https://doi.org/10.11648/j.ajsea.20241201.12

Kasturi, S., Li, X., Li, P., & Pickard, J. (2024d). Predicting Attack Paths from Application Security Vulnerabilities Using a Multi-Layer Perceptron. In *American Journal of Software Engineering and Applications,* 2024, Vol. 12, No. 1, pp. 23-35, https://doi.org/10.11648/j.ajsea.20241201.14

Kubasek, N.K., Brennan, B. A., & Browne, N.M. (2017). The Legal Environment of Business – A Critical Thinking Approach, *Pearson*

Kurose, J.F., & Ross, K.W. (2017). Computer Networking: A Top Down Approach, *7th Edition, Pearson, 2017*

Lohmann, P., Albuquerque, C., & Machado, R.C.S. (2023). "Systematic Literature Review of Threat Modeling Concepts", In *Proceedings of the 9th International Conference on Information Systems Security and Privacy - ICISSP*; ISBN 978-989-758-624-8; ISSN 2184-4356, SciTePress, pages 163-173. DOI: 10.5220/0011783000003405, February 22-24, 2023, in Lisbon, Portugal Available from: http://dx.doi.org/10.5220/0000168400003405, SciTePress - Publication Details

Lindstrom, P. (2022). Cybersecurity metrics corporate boards want to see, CSO, *https://www.csoonline.com/article/572603/cybersecurity-metrics-corporate-boards-want-to-see.html*

Miller, D., Harris, S., Harper, A., Van Dyke, S., Blask, C. (2010). Security Information and Event Management (SIEM) Implementation; *McGraw Hill: New York, NY, USA, 2010.*

MITRE, (2018). Common Vulnerabilities and Exposures (CVE) Numbering Authority (CNA) Rules, *MITRE, https://cve.mitre.org/cve/cna/CNA_Rules_v2.0.pdf*

https://nvd.nist.gov/vuln

MITRE, (2022). 2022 CWE Top 25 Most Dangerous Software Weaknesses, *MITRE, https://cwe.mitre.org/top25/archive/2021/2021_cwe_top25.html*

MITRE. (2023a). 2023 On the Cusp-Other Dangerous Software Weaknesses. *MITRE*, Available from: CWE - 2023 On the Cusp - Other Dangerous Software Weaknesses (mitre.org)

MITRE. (2023b). CWE Top 25 Most Dangerous Software Weaknesses. *MITRE*, Available from: CWE - 2023 CWE Top 25 Most Dangerous Software Weaknesses (mitre.org)

Morgan, S. (2021). 10 Hot Security Ratings Companies To Watch In 2021, *Cybercrime Magazine, https://cybersecurityventures.com/security-ratings-companies/*

Na, J. (2021). Introducing Secure Application: True Runtime Application Self-Protection (RASP) for the Modern Application, *CISCO App Dynamics, https://www.appdynamics.com/blog/product/application-security/*

OWASP, (2021). OWASP Top 10, *OWASP, https://owasp.org/Top10/*

OWASP-API, (2023). OWASP API Security Top 10, *OWASP, https://owasp.org/API-Security/editions/2023/en/0xa2-broken-authentication/*

Primeon, (2018). Enterprise Applications: Wide Open to Attack in 2018, *Primeon, https://www.primeon.com/whitepaper/primeon_wp2_r.pdf?1*

Reversing Labs. (2023). How to Evaluate Threat Intelligence Feeds, *eBook-How-to-Evaluate-Threat-Intelligence-Feeds PDF (www.reversinglabs.com)*

Saini, V., Duan, Q., & Paruchuri, V. (2008). Threat modeling using attack trees. *Journal of Computing Sciences in Colleges, 23*, 124-131, Available from: (PDF) Threat Modeling Using Attack Trees (researchgate.net)

Salemi, M. (2020). Automated rules generation into Web Application Firewall using Runtime Application Self-Protection. *Ecole polytechnique de Louvain, Université catholique de Louvain, 2020. Prom.:Ramin Sadre; Legay, Axel.* Available from: Automated rules generation into Web Application Firewall using Runtime Application Self-Protection | Mémoire UCL (uclouvain.be)

SALT, (2023). State of API Security Q1 2023, *SALT LABS*

Sevri, M., & Karacan, H. (2019). Deep learning-based web application security. Proc. of 2nd Int. Conf. on Advanced Technologies, in *Proc. Computer Engineering and Science (ICATCES), Antalya, Turkey, pp. 349-354, Apr. 2019.*

Smith, Gambrell., & Russell, LLP. (2016). Data Breaches, *Smith, Gambrell, & Russell LLP, Summer 2016.*

Shey, H. (2023). The Forrester Wave™: Data Security Platforms, Q1 2023, *Forrester, https://reprints2.forrester.com/#/assets/2/424/RES178465/report*

Signal Sciences, (2021). Identifying Web Attack Indicators, *https://info.signalsciences.com/identify-web-attack-indicators*

Veracode, (2019). State Of Software Security Vol. 10, *Veracode https://www.veracode.com/sites/default/files/pdf/resources/sossreports/state-of-software-security-volume-10-veracode-report.pdf*

Veracode, (2022). State Of Software Security Vol. 12, *Veracode https://www.veracode.com/sites/default/files/pdf/resources/sossreports/state-of-software-security-v12-nwm.pdf*

Veracode, (2023). State Of Software Security Vol. 13, *Veracode https://www.veracode.com/state-of-software-security-report*

Warner, R.M. (2020). Applied Statistics – II Multivariable and Multivariate Techniques, *SAGE Publications*

White, R., & Donahue, D. (2014). Art of Network Architecture, The: Business-Driven Design (Networking Technology) *1st Edition, CISCO Press., April 4, 2014*

Xiong, W., Legrand, E., Aberg, O., & Lagerstrom, R. (2022). Cyber security threat modeling based on the MITRE Enterprise ATT&CK Matrix. *Software and Systems Modeling (2022) 21:157–177* https://doi.org/10.1007/s10270-021-00898-7

Appendix: Additional Reading

Global Cybersecurity Landscape 2024: Threats, Trends, and Resilience

Comprehensive Data-Driven Analysis, Industry Insights, and Best Practices

Executive Overview

This section provides a high-level summary of the cybersecurity landscape in 2024, highlighting unprecedented adversarial innovation, the rise of sophisticated attack vectors, and the necessity for organization-wide resilience and adaptability. Year 2024 marked a pivotal year in cybersecurity, defined by the convergence of advanced adversarial tactics, AI-driven threats, and increasing regulatory pressures. Ransomware, supply chain attacks, and phishing remain dominant, while emerging risks like AI-powered malware and quantum computing loom on the horizon. This chapter frames the urgency for a proactive, intelligence-driven defense posture.

The Modern Threat Landscape

This section synthesizes findings from leading industry reports (CrowdStrike, 2024; Fortinet, 2024; Palo Alto Networks, 2024; SecurityScorecard, 2024; BitSight, 2024; IBM, 2024; Qualys, 2024; Veracode, 2024) to paint a comprehensive picture of current cyber threats.

- Ransomware continues to be the most disruptive and costly attack type, with double and triple extortion tactics (CrowdStrike, 2024; Fortinet 2024; SecurityScorecard, 2024).
- Supply chain and third-party risks are surging, as attackers exploit software dependencies and vendor relationships (Fortinet 2024; SecurityScorecard, 2024; BitSight, 2024).
- Phishing and social engineering attacks have evolved through AI-generated lures and deepfakes (Palo Alto Networks, 2024; Fortinet, 2024).
- Nation-state and APT groups are expanding in scale and sophistication, with zero-day exploits and persistent infiltration (CrowdStrike, 2024; Palo Alto Networks, 2024).

- Cloud misconfiguration and IoT vulnerabilities are primary attack vectors due to increased digital transformation (Fortinet, 2024, Palo Alto Networks 2024; Qualys, 2024).

The threat landscape is characterized by relentless innovation from adversaries, with increases in ransomware, phishing, and supply chain attacks. Emerging technologies, while empowering defense—also introduce new risks.

Sectoral and Regional Analysis

This section examines industry-specific trends and geographic distinctions, drawing on data from (SecurityScorecard, 2024; BitSight 2024; and IBM, 2024).

- Healthcare: Highest average breach cost ($10.9M/incident), persistent ransomware and data extortion, challenges with legacy systems (IBM, 2024; BitSight, 2024).
- Financial Services: Strongest overall security posture, but targets for credential theft, BEC, and fintech attacks (BitSight, 2024; SecurityScorecard, 2024).
- Manufacturing & Retail: Supply chain vulnerabilities and ransomware dominate, particularly for mid-sized firms (BitSight, 2024; SecurityScorecard, 2024).
- Energy & Utilities: Operational technology (OT) at risk from nation-state actors and ransomware (CrowdStrike, 2024; Fortinet, 2024; SecurityScorecard, 2024).
- Regional Trends: North America (highest incident disclosure, mature regulations), Europe (regulatory focus, cross-border challenges), APAC (growth in nation-state threats, resource constraints), Latin America & Africa (infrastructure and awareness gaps) (SecurityScorecard, 2024; BitSight, 2024).

Cyber risk and readiness vary significantly across sectors and regions; healthcare and critical infrastructure face the greatest challenges, while regulatory environments drive improvement but also expose gaps.

Attack Vectors and Emerging Tactics

A deep dive into the main methods adversaries use, with statistics and technical analysis.

- Ransomware: 40% rise in attacks over 2023, median dwell time eight days (CrowdStrike, 2024; IBM, 2024).
- Phishing & Social Engineering: 40% increase in AI-driven campaigns, deepfake-enabled fraud (Fortinet, 2024; Palo Alto Networks, 2024; SecurityScorecard, 2024).
- Zero-Day Exploits: Record-high exploitation rates, with the average exploitation time less than 48 hours after disclosure (CrowdStrike, 2024; Palo Alto Networks, 2024).
- Credential Theft: Implicated in 41% of major breaches (BitSight).
- Living-off-the-Land and AI-Powered Malware: Adversaries use legitimate admin tools and self-learning malware for evasion (Fortinet, 2024; Palo Alto Networks, 2024).
- Cloud and IoT Attacks: Misconfiguration and weak identity controls continue to expose sensitive data (Fortinet, 2024; Qualys, 2024; Palo Alto Networks, 2024).

Attackers are leveraging automation, AI, and rapidly shifting vectors to compromise targets, requiring organizations to adopt multi-layered and adaptive defense strategies.

Key Cybersecurity Solutions and Best Practices

This section compiles best practices and solutions advocated across leading reports.

- Zero Trust Architecture: "Never trust, always verify" approach, continuous authentication, and micro-segmentation (CrowdStrike, 2024; Fortinet, 2024; SecurityScorecard, 2024).
- Security Awareness Training: Essential for defense against phishing and social engineering (Fortinet, 2024; IBM, 2024; Palo Alto Networks, 2024).
- Continuous Monitoring & Threat Intelligence: Real-time feeds and automated detection (CrowdStrike, 2024; BitSight, 2024; SecurityScorecard, 2024).

- Automated Vulnerability Management: Rapid identification, prioritization, and remediation (Qualys, 2024; Veracode, 2024; BitSight, 2024).
- Incident Response Planning: Regular exercises, clear communication, and integration with third parties (IBM, 2024; BitSight, 2024; SecurityScorecard, 2024).
- Vendor & Supply Chain Risk Management: Continuous assessment and contractual security requirements (SecurityScorecard, 2024; BitSight, 2024).

Proactive investment in technology, training, and process automation is vital for reducing risk and operationalizing cyber resilience.

Case Studies and Real-World Impact

Select case studies from the referenced reports illustrate the real-world impact of cybersecurity best practices and failures.

- Financial Services Firm: Reduced average vendor risk score by 14% in six months through daily monitoring alerts (BitSight, 2024).
- Healthcare Network: Cut critical vulnerabilities by 37% and improved cyber risk score by 62 points with improved patch management (BitSight, 2024; Qualys, 2024).
- Retailer: 24% reduction in security incidents after implementing continuous monitoring and training (BitSight, 2024).
- Healthcare Ransomware Attack: Multi-million-dollar ransom averted with swift incident containment and forensics (Palo Alto Networks, 2024).
- Supply Chain Compromise: Coordinated response to software vendor attack highlighted value of secure SDLC and continuous monitoring (Palo Alto Networks, 2024; SecurityScorecard, 2024).

Organizations that embrace real-time monitoring, automation, and layered defense see measurable improvements in risk reduction and breach containment.

Future Trends and Strategic Recommendations

A forward-looking discussion of evolving threats and recommended strategies.

- AI Arms Race: Both defenders and adversaries leveraging AI; ethical AI and human oversight are critical (CrowdStrike, 2024; Fortinet,2024; SecurityScorecard, 2024).
- Quantum Computing: Impending risk to encryption standards, necessitating quantum-resistant cryptography (Fortinet, 2024).
- Regulatory Expansion: Stricter global regulations on breach disclosure and
- privacy driving security investments (BitSight, 2024; SecurityScorecard, 2024).
- Cyber Insurance: Tighter underwriting standards; aligning security controls with insurance requirements (SecurityScorecard, 2024).
- Integrated Security Operations: Convergence of vulnerability management, threat detection, and compliance (Qualys, 2024; Veracode, 2024).

The future demands agility, automation, and cross-sector collaboration as cyber risks escalate and technologies—and regulations—continue to evolve.

Executive Summary: Cybersecurity Landscape 2024

In 2024, the cybersecurity landscape is more complex and challenging than ever. Ransomware, phishing, and supply chain attacks have become the most frequent and damaging threats, with attackers using increasingly advanced tactics, including AI-driven scams and exploiting software vendors. Sectors such as healthcare and critical infrastructure are particularly at risk, often facing the highest costs and disruption.

Businesses worldwide are responding with strategies centered on zero trust, automation, and continuous monitoring. Training employees to recognize and respond to threats remains one of the most effective defenses, alongside well-developed incident response plans. Automated vulnerability management and real-time threat intelligence are also playing crucial roles in detection and prevention.

Different regions and industries face unique risks. For example, healthcare organizations often deal with legacy systems and have some of the highest breach costs, while financial firms are prime targets for credential theft and business email compromise. Meanwhile, regulatory requirements continue to evolve, especially in North America and Europe, driving improvements in security but also creating new challenges.

Emerging risks include AI-powered malware, quantum computing's potential to break encryption, and increasing pressure from cyber insurance providers to meet higher security standards. Case studies from 2024 show that organizations investing in continuous monitoring, automation, and layered defenses are better at reducing incidents and recovering from attacks.

Looking ahead, cybersecurity will require ongoing adaptation. The use of AI and automation will increase on both sides—among defenders and attackers—while regulatory frameworks and technologies rapidly evolve. Collaboration, proactive investment, and a focus on resilience will be essential for organizations aiming to stay ahead of these threats.

Key Takeaways from the 2024 Cybersecurity Landscape

- Ransomware, phishing, and supply chain attacks remain the most prevalent and costly threats—attackers are employing increasingly advanced tactics, including AI-driven scams and exploitation of vendor relationships.
- Sector-specific risks demand tailored responses: Healthcare and critical infrastructure face the highest breach costs and disruption, largely due to legacy systems and operational vulnerabilities.
- Automation and AI are shaping both attack and defense strategies, with adversaries leveraging cutting-edge tools while organizations boost detection, prevention, and response capabilities through automation and real-time monitoring.
- Security awareness training and robust incident response plans are essential defenses—preparing employees to identify threats and respond quickly greatly reduces organizational risk.
- Regulatory changes, especially in North America and Europe, drive improvements in security practices but also pose new compliance challenges for businesses.

- Emerging risks, such as quantum computing and AI-powered malware, necessitate proactive investment in new defensive technologies, process adaptation, and ongoing collaboration across sectors.
- Organizations with layered defenses, continuous monitoring, and automated vulnerability management show measurable improvements in risk mitigation and recovery following cyber incidents.
- Looking ahead, ongoing adaptation, resilience, and collaboration will be critical as the cyber threat landscape grows ever more complex and fast evolving.

Comprehension and Discussion Questions: Cybersecurity Landscape 2024

Analyzing Threats, Trends, and Strategic Responses

Comprehension Questions

- According to the overview, what are the most prevalent and costly types of cyber threats in 2024?
- List at least three emerging risks mentioned in the summary and briefly describe why they are significant.
- Which sectors are identified as facing the highest breach costs and disruption, and what are the primary reasons for their increased vulnerability?
- How are automation and artificial intelligence shaping both attack and defense strategies in the cybersecurity landscape?
- What is the role of regulatory changes in North America and Europe in shaping organizational cybersecurity practices?
- According to real-world case studies, what measurable improvements have organizations seen after adopting automation and layered defenses?
- What is the importance of security awareness training and incident response plans as highlighted in the summary?
- Why is continuous monitoring particularly crucial for organizations aiming to mitigate risk?

Discussion Questions

- Given the growing sophistication of AI-driven attacks, what ethical challenges might arise in the use of AI for both attackers and defenders?
- How can organizations in industries with legacy systems (such as healthcare or critical infrastructure) balance operational requirements with the need to upgrade cybersecurity defenses?
- In the context of increasing regulatory requirements, what strategies can organizations use to ensure compliance without stifling innovation?
- What are the potential impacts of quantum computing on current encryption standards, and how should organizations begin to prepare?
- Discuss the benefits and potential challenges of adopting a Zero Trust Architecture across diverse organizational environments.
- How can cross-sector collaboration and information sharing contribute to a more resilient global cybersecurity posture?
- Reflecting on the case studies, what common factors contributed to successful risk reduction and incident response?
- What role should cyber insurance play in an organization's overall risk management and security strategy?

Citations

- Qualys. (2024). Vulnerability Management Whitepaper, https://cdn2.qualys.com/docs/mktg/whitepapers/best-practices-selecting-vulnerability-management-solution.pdf
- Checkmarx. (2024). Secure Code Review Best Practices, https://checkmarx.com/learn/developers/secure-code-review-6-best-practices-every-developer-should-follow/
- IBM Security. (2024). Cost of a Data Breach Report, https://www.ibm.com/think/insights/cost-of-a-data-breach-2024-financial-industry.
- CrowdStrike. (2024). Global Threat Report 2024, https://www.crowdstrike.com/enus/resources/reports/crowdstrike2024global-threat-report/
- Fortinet. (2024). 2024 Cybersecurity Threat Landscape Report, https://www.fortinet.com/content/dam/fortinet/assets/threat-reports/threat-landscape-report-2h-2023.pdf
- Palo Alto Networks Unit 42. (2025). Threat Intelligence Report, https://www.paloaltonetworks.com/unit42
- SecurityScorecard. (2024). Global Cyber Risk Insights Report, https://securityscorecard.com/blog/2024-global-third-party-cybersecurity-breach-report/#:~:text=SecurityScorecard%20threat%20analysts%20found%20that,breaches%20by%20a%20similar%20margin
- BitSight. (2024). Cyber Risk Ratings 2024, https://www.bitsight.com/blog/2024-bitsight-ratings-algorithm-update-purpose-observations-and-impact#:~:text=As%20our%202024%20Rating%20Algorithm,utility%20of%20the%20ratings%20by.
- Veracode. (2024). State of Software Security Report, https://www.veracode.com/state-software-security-2024-report/

Comprehensive Analysis of Top 20 Cybersecurity Attacks: Vectors, Prevalence, and Readiness in 2024

Global Statistics, Attack Pathways, and Preparedness — A Data-Driven Report

Introduction

The cybersecurity landscape in 2024 is more dynamic and perilous than ever, with threat actors leveraging sophisticated tactics to exploit vulnerabilities across organizations, industries, and geographic regions. This report synthesizes data from leading industry sources to present a comprehensive overview of the top 20 most prevalent cybersecurity attacks. Each attack type is examined in detail, including its main attack vectors, global prevalence, statistical impact, and the state of organizational readiness. Figures and tables are provided to illustrate key trends, with all sources cited for transparency and verification.

Top 20 Cybersecurity Attacks in 2024

Rank	Attack Type	Primary Attack Vectors	Global Prevalence (%)	Avg. Cost per Incident (USD)	Organizational Readiness (Score/10)
1	Ransomware	Phishing, Remote Desktop Protocol (RDP), Software Vulnerabilities	24	$5.3M	6.2
2	Phishing/Spear Phishing	Email, Social Engineering, Malicious Links/Attachments	41	$3.8M	6.8
3	Business Email Compromise (BEC)	Email Spoofing, Social Engineering	17	$4.6M	5.9
4	Supply Chain Attacks	Third-Party Software, Vendor Compromise	20	$4.2M	5.7

5	Credential Theft/Account Takeover	Phishing, Brute Force, Password Spray	32	$2.9M	5.5
6	Denial of Service (DoS/DDoS)	Botnets, Amplification Attacks	14	$1.8M	6.0
7	Malware (General)	Email, Drive-by Download, Removable Media	36	$2.7M	6.3
8	Zero-Day Exploits	Unpatched Vulnerabilities, Drive-by attacks	11	$4.9M	4.8
9	SQL Injection	Web Application Inputs, Vulnerable APIs	7	$2.1M	5.5
10	Cross-Site Scripting (XSS)	Compromised Web Forms, Malicious Scripts	9	$1.6M	5.4
11	Man-in-the-Middle (MitM)	Insecure Wi-Fi, Session Hijacking	6	$2.2M	5.7
12	Cloud Misconfiguration	Open Buckets, Mismanaged Permissions	13	$3.6M	4.9
13	Insider Threats	Disgruntled Employees, Negligence	8	$4.5M	5.3
14	IoT Attacks	Default Credentials, Unpatched Firmware	12	$1.4M	4.6
15	Advanced Persistent Threats (APT)	Zero-Days, Social Engineering, Lateral Movement	5	$7.8M	5.1
16	Social Engineering (non-phishing)	Phone, In-person, Impersonation	10	$1.1M	5.8
17	Drive-by Downloads	Compromised Websites, Malvertising	9	$1.3M	5.6
18	Data Exfiltration	Malware, Insider Actions, Cloud Storage	7	$3.2M	5.2

19	Cryptojacking	Browser Scripts, Malicious Containers	4	$950K	5.0
20	Deepfake and AI-enabled Attacks	AI-generated Phishing, Social Engineering	3	$1.5M	4.4

Sources: IBM Security (2024), CrowdStrike Global Threat Report (2024), Fortinet Threat Landscape Report (2024), Palo Alto Networks Unit 42 (2024), Veracode SoSS (2024), BitSight Cyber Risk Ratings (2024), SecurityScorecard Global Insights (2024).

Attack Vectors: In-Depth Analysis

- Ransomware: Phishing remains the predominant vector, with attackers increasingly exploiting remote desktop weaknesses and unpatched software. Globally, ransomware accounts for 24% of all breaches, with an average cost exceeding $5.3M per incident (IBM, 2024).
- Phishing/Spear Phishing: Sophisticated email lures, often AI-generated, topped 41% prevalence globally; readiness is improving but remains reactive (SecurityScorecard, 2024).
- Supply Chain Attacks: Targeting software and hardware providers, attackers inserting malicious code or compromise credentials. These incidents now cause 20% of breaches worldwide and often cascade into hundreds of organizations (Fortinet, 2024).
- Credential Theft/Account Takeover: Compromised credentials were the root cause of 32% of major breaches, with brute force and phishing as leading tactics (BitSight, 2024).
- Cloud Misconfiguration: 13% of breaches stemmed from misconfigured cloud resources, especially open storage and excessive privileges (Palo Alto Networks, 2025).
- Zero-Day Exploits: 2024 saw an all-time high in zero-day exploitation, with attackers leveraging unpatched flaws before disclosure (CrowdStrike, 2024).
- IoT Attacks: Attacks targeting IoT grew by 12%, fueled by default credentials and unpatched firmware (Fortinet, 2024).
- Deepfake and AI-enabled Attacks: Though representing 3% of attacks, the impact of deepfake scams is rapidly growing, especially in financial fraud and executive impersonation (SecurityScorecard, 2024).

Global Prevalence and Impact

Global Prevalence of Top Cybersecurity Attacks in 2024, Ransomware, phishing, malware, and credential theft dominate by frequency and financial impact are all detailed in references sourced in this section. Source: IBM Security, 2024; CrowdStrike, 2024.

According to the IBM Cost of a Data Breach Report (2024), the average cost of a breach has reached $4.45 million globally, with healthcare experiencing the highest sectoral impact (over $10.9 million per breach). Ransomware and supply chain attacks, in particular, exhibit year-over-year growth, expanding in both complexity and reach. Attackers are exploiting the surge in remote work and cloud adoption, targeting weak links in organizational defenses.

Organizational Readiness

Average Organizational Readiness Scores by Attack Type (out of 10) reflect maturity of detection, prevention, and response capabilities. Source: BitSight, 2024; SecurityScorecard, 2024.

Organizations with mature automation, incident response, and employee training report cost savings of up to $1.76 million per breach (IBM, 2024). Yet, readiness remains variable: while sectors like financial services and technology lead in prevention maturity, healthcare and retail lag, often due to legacy infrastructure and resource constraints.

Summary: Top 20 Cybersecurity Attacks in 2024

The 2024 cybersecurity landscape is marked by increasingly sophisticated and frequent attacks targeting organizations worldwide. Key findings from industry leaders reveal the following trends:

- Ransomware, phishing, and credential theft are among the most prevalent attacks, causing significant financial losses and operational disruption.
- Supply chain attacks continue to rise, affecting a growing number of organizations through third-party vulnerabilities.

- Cloud misconfigurations and zero-day exploits have surged, highlighting weaknesses in cloud adoption and delay in patching new threats.
- Business email compromise and social engineering remain highly effective, exploiting human error and trust to bypass technical defenses.
- Emerging threats like deepfake and AI-enabled attacks, as well as IoT exploits, are becoming more common, signaling a shift in attacker tactics.

The average cost of a data breach has climbed to $4.45 million globally, with industries such as healthcare being especially vulnerable. Organizational readiness varies: companies investing in automation, incident response, and employee training see notably lower costs and faster recovery.

Sources: IBM Security (2024), CrowdStrike (2024), Fortinet (2024), Palo Alto Networks (2025), Veracode, BitSight, and SecurityScorecard.

Key Takeaways: Top 20 Cybersecurity Attacks in 2024

- Ransomware, phishing, and credential theft remain the most common and damaging cyberattacks, responsible for major financial and operational harm worldwide.
- Supply chain vulnerabilities and cloud misconfigurations are driving new waves of widespread breaches, affecting organizations through third-party dependencies and rapid cloud adoption.
- Zero-day exploits and advanced persistent threats (APTs) are on the rise, reflecting the increasing sophistication of attackers and the urgency for timely patching and threat intelligence.
- Business email compromise, social engineering, and the emergence of deep-fake and AI-enabled attacks highlight that human factors are still a critical weak point in many defenses.
- Industries such as healthcare face the highest average cost per breach, with the global average now at $4.45 million, underscoring the need for sector-specific strategies.
- Organizations investing in security automation, incident response planning, and employee training experience lower breach costs and faster recovery times.

- Despite growing threats, organizational readiness varies widely: sectors with mature prevention and response capabilities fare significantly better than those with legacy systems and limited resources.
- Continuous monitoring, proactive risk management, and robust third-party oversight are essential to adapt to the evolving cybersecurity threat landscape in 2024.

Comprehension and Discussion Questions: Top 20 Cybersecurity Attacks in 2024

Comprehension Questions

- According to the report, which three types of cyberattacks are responsible for the most widespread financial and operational harm in 2024?
- What are the main factors driving the increase in supply chain attacks and cloud misconfigurations?
- Which attack vector has the highest global prevalence, and what is its percentage?
- What is the average cost of a data breach in 2024, and which industry faces the highest costs per incident?
- How have zero-day exploits and advanced persistent threats (APTs) evolved, and why are organizations particularly concerned about these threats?
- What are the key attack vectors for credential theft and account takeover incidents?
- According to the organizational readiness scores, which sectors are best prepared to respond to cyber threats, and which are lagging?
- What specific strategies are linked to lower breach costs and faster recovery times?
- How prevalent are deep-fake and AI-enabled attacks, and why are they considered a growing concern?

Discussion Questions

- Discuss the impact of cloud adoption and remote work trends on the cybersecurity posture of organizations. What new risks have emerged as a result?
- How can organizations balance the need for rapid digital transformation with the requirement for robust cybersecurity measures?
- In what ways do human factors continue to undermine cybersecurity defenses, despite advances in technology?
- Reflect on the role of continuous monitoring and third-party oversight in reducing organizational risk. What challenges might companies face in implementing these practices effectively?
- Consider the rise of AI-enabled attacks such as deepfakes. What ethical and operational questions do these new threat types pose for both attackers and defenders?
- Given the statistical evidence, where should organizations prioritize their cybersecurity investments in 2024, and why?
- Evaluate the effectiveness of current incident response strategies based on the data presented. What improvements would you recommend?

Sources

- IBM Security. (2024). Cost of a Data Breach Report, https://www.ibm.com/think/insights/cost-of-a-data-breach-2024-financial-industry.
- CrowdStrike. (2024). Global Threat Report 2024, https://www.crowdstrike.com/en-us/resources/reports/crowdstrike-2024-global-threat-report/
- Fortinet. (2024). 2024 Cybersecurity Threat Landscape Report, https://www.fortinet.com/content/dam/fortinet/assets/threat-reports/threat-landscape-report-2h-2023.pdf
- Palo Alto Networks Unit 42. (2025). Threat Intelligence Report, https://www.paloaltonetworks.com/unit42
- SecurityScorecard. (2024). Global Cyber Risk Insights Report, https://securityscorecard.com/blog/2024-global-third-party-cybersecurity-breach-report/#:~:text=SecurityScorecard%20threat%20analysts%20found%20that,breaches%20by%20a%20similar%20margin
- BitSight. (2024). Cyber Risk Ratings 2024, https://www.bitsight.com/blog/2024-bitsightratingsalgorithmupdatepurpose-observationsandimpact#:~:text=As%20our%202024%20Rating%20Algorithm,utility%20of%20the%20ratings%20by.
- Veracode. (2024). State of Software Security Report, https://www.veracode.com/state-software-security-2024-report/

Recommended Additional References

Extending the Research Foundation in Cybersecurity

- Bada, M., Sasse, M. A., & Nurse, J. R. C. (2019). Cyber security awareness campaigns: Why do they fail to change behavior? Computers & Security, 87, 101-123, https://doi.org/10.48550/arXiv.1901.02672
- Chen, T. M., & Abu-Nimeh, S. (2011). Lessons from Stuxnet. Computer, 44(4), 91-93. DOI: 10.1109/MC.2011.115, https://ieeexplore.ieee.org/document/5742014
- ENISA. (2024). ENISA Threat Landscape 2024. European Union Agency for Cybersecurity, https://www.enisa.europa.eu/publications/enisa-threat-landscape-2024.
- Singer, P.W., & Friedman, A. (2022). Cybersecurity and Cyberwar: What Everyone Needs to Know (2nd ed.). Oxford University Press, https://global.oup.com/academic/product/cybersecurity-and-cyberwar-9780199918119?cc=us&lang=en&; ISBN-10: 9780199918119, ISBN-13: 978-0199918119
- Jang-Jaccard, J., & Nepal, S. (2014). A survey of emerging threats in cybersecurity. Journal of Computer and System Sciences, 80(5), 973-993, https://doi.org/10.1016/j.jcss.2014.02.005
- Krebs, B. (2023). Spam Nation: The Inside Story of Organized Cybercrime—from Global Epidemic to Your Front Door. Sourcebooks, ISBN-13 978-1402295614.
- National Institute of Standards and Technology. (2024). Framework for Improving Critical Infrastructure Cybersecurity (Version 2.0), https://doi.org/10.6028/NIST.CSWP.29
- Perlroth, N. (2021). This Is How They Tell Me the World Ends: The Cyberweapons Arms Race. Bloomsbury Publishing, ISBN 9781635576061, https://www.bloomsbury.com/us/this-is-how-they-tell-me-the-world-ends-9781635576061/
- Shackelford, S. J. (2022). Managing Cyber Attacks in International Law, Business, and Relations: In Search of Cyber Peace (2nd ed.). Cambridge University Press, ISBN-10 1107004373, ISBN-13 978-1107004375

Index

www.ingramcontent.com/pod-product-compliance
Lightning Source LLC
LaVergne TN
LVHW022045200926
848481LV00003B/794
* 9 7 9 8 8 9 9 6 6 1 8 4 6 *